The **Independent School Gove**

Edited by Andrew Maiden

First edition

© pentastic ltd November 2009

ISBN 978-0-9563092-0-4

Many thanks to Marsh Ltd, Education Practice for their
sponsorship of this book: **www.marsh.co.uk**

Acknowledgements

Design: Liz Gilbert. Liz can be contacted on
liz@lizgilbertdesign.co.uk

Index: Caroline Wilding. Caroline can be contacted
on **cw@cwilding.com**

Print: Constructive Media

Proofing/amends and comments:
Giles Bowring (bursar, Giggleswick School),

Clive Gutteridge (bursar, Appleford School),

Tim Holgate (former director of training
at the Boarding Schools' Association),

Nigel Richardson (former chairman of
The Headmasters' and Headmistresses'
Conference and former head of the Perse School), and

Dr Anthony Seldon (master, Wellington College).

Many thanks to them for their input.

Introduction

Independent schools in the UK are leading the way in the quality of educational provision. Many schools are exporting this excellence by franchising their school's expertise throughout the world. Meanwhile, growing numbers of pupils from overseas are attending British boarding schools. In effect, independent schools are waving the flag for UK plc.

Political whims and economic challenges are putting more pressure on independent schools to maintain their high standards. While the numbers of pupils studying science and languages are diminishing in the state sector, the independent sector flourishes in these areas and also continues to produce leaders in British society, not least in politics, business, scientific innovation and sport. It is a pity that these successes are too little recognised at home.

The role of the independent school governor is changing too. Gone are the days when a governor merely had to turn up occasionally and nod through proposals made by the head and/or bursar. They now play an increasingly important part in running the school.

They are responsible for the school's legal and regulatory compliance, strategic direction, assets and standards. The demands may be greater now, but they can be more fulfilling too.

Most independent schools are charities (approximately 80 per cent of sector pupils are taught in them), with the remainder run by proprietors. The latter group, as profit-making entities, do not require governing bodies. So, for our purposes, when we use the term "independent schools", we generally mean the charitable form. However, we have included some information specific to proprietor-owned schools, since some enlist advisory boards that act in a similar way to governing bodies.

This book is designed to help you, the governor, to understand and appreciate the scope of your role; but also to think more broadly about your school from a strategic and financial perspective to give you the opportunity to become more than a critical friend: in fact, an active supporter.

The references to laws in this handbook apply mainly to England and Wales, but other issues of good governance are still relevant to schools in Scotland and Northern Ireland.

Andrew Maiden
Editor

Contents

Chapter **1**

The governing body: its role, composition, induction of new governors, the chair, the clerk, meetings, sub-committees: by Andrew Maiden

The governing body sets out the aims of the school and ensures that they are met, in conjunction with the headteacher. These policies, plans and procedures are designed to at least maintain and improve the education of the pupils on the school roll. This should be achieved within the financial constraints of the school.

Every charitable independent school has a governing document, which could be a trust deed, article of government or a memorandum and articles of a company. The governing body must ensure that the school follows these requirements to the letter and adopts legislation affecting the sector.

Governors are also trustees of the charity (the school). This means that there may be an additional responsibility to preserve endowments, maintain property and ensure the solvency of the charity. If the school has been set up as a company, there will be requirements to conform to company legislation (see the chapter on key legislation). Governors may also be personally liable in either instance (see the chapter on governor liabilities). Governors should be adults of reasonable experience.

The precise legal position for governors of charitable independent schools' responsibilities is covered in the chapter on key legislation. What follows here is general guidance that applies to all independent schools with a governing body and, in some instances, an advisory board (in the case of a proprieter-owned school).

Composition

Some governors will have been selected for their specific talents eg knowledge of finance or property. However, the governing body is not expected to have expertise in all disciplines for running a school most effectively. There will be many occasions when external professional advice must be sought.

The governing body should ideally have a range of skills that broadly covers key areas:
- a financial expert or someone with a background in business;
- a retired head and/or bursar;
- a teacher or educationalist (a teacher from a similar school or university, or an inspector);
- parents at the school; and
- others from certain professions: law, architecture/building/estates management, marketing/fundraising etc would all be useful.

Some schools have a development director. It is useful to invite her or him to particular meetings to make presentations on fundraising, where appropriate.

Governing bodies usually number between 10 and 24, depending on the size of the school, but an ideal grouping is 14 or 15, otherwise the decision-making process can become bogged down in endless debate. However, a bigger governing body allows greater flexibility if setting up sub-committees or working parties for various projects. These two sets of bodies can manage aspects of the governing body's work on its behalf and report back to the full governing body on progress.

Governors must act impartially, as "critical friends" and, in particular, parent governors must not lobby on behalf of their child or their child's class over some matter. They must act in the interests of the school as a whole, but can give general feedback to colleagues on the governing body about how the school is perceived by other parents. However, they should not be viewed by parents as their representatives.

A balance between men and women is also desirable. In addition, if the school has a high representation of pupils from ethnic minorities or particular religious beliefs, it is advantageous to have a governor who shares that ethnicity or religion; not as an advocate, but to properly reflect the nature of the school.

A list of governors should be made available in the school prospectus, newsletter and website. Parents or other interested parties should be able to contact the governing body through the clerk to the governors, usually care of the school.

Since continuity is important, particularly for long-term school building projects, governors are usually expected to serve for (renewable) terms of five years. However, it is important that the composition of personalities is refreshed reasonably often to avoid the decision-making process becoming stale or that innovation is thwarted to avoid change. Above all, it is important to avoid comments such as "that's not how we do things" to new suggestions.

Potential conflicts of interest should always be announced by individual governors and recorded by the governing body.

Responsibility to parents

A parent contract clarifies parents' obligations for paying fees and observance by their children of the school rules. In return, the school provides a quality of education and pastoral care. The contract also sets out steps for breach of contract for both parties. If the parents make a complaint to the school, a panel of governors (plus an independent individual) is assembled to hear the alleged grievance. The governors must act impartially, and according to the school's formal complaints procedure.

The terms of the contract should be outlined in the school prospectus.

The school's statutory accounts must be made openly available to parents. This helps establish fair reasons behind the fees payable, creating a greater sense of rapport and understanding between parents and the school.

Induction

Becoming a governor can be a daunting experience. The history of the school, coupled with the experience of other governors, plus the responsibility of overseeing the effective education of pupils, can all make the role appear challenging. Well, it is. However, it is also extremely rewarding and can provide a governor with new skills that they can use in other areas of their professional lives.

A new governor should be mentored by a current governor. They should also be given details of courses run by the Association of Governing Bodies of Independent Schools (see **www.agbis.info**).

Important documents for a new governor:
- school constitution/governing documents;
- school development plan;
- leaflets CC3 The Essential Trustee and CC10 The Hallmarks of an Effective Charity, both from the Charity Commission;
- minutes from the previous six months' meetings (including sub-committees' reports);
- most recent governors' report and accounts;
- most recent inspection report;
- list of school policies;
- staff handbook;
- current school prospectus/website address;
- guide to educational jargon;
- planned meeting dates for the rest of the academic year;
- most recent school newsletter/magazine;
- other governors' contact information;
- full staff list; and
- a copy of The Independent School Governor's Handbook.

The chair

The chair of the governing body is key to its success. S/he should have held office on the governing body for some years. S/he is elected by the other governors, usually on an annual basis.

The chair runs the agenda (set by the clerk, in conjunction with the chair, head and bursar). S/he ensures that the business of the meetings is run professionally, that everyone has the opportunity to speak and that the governors work together as a team. S/he leads in supporting and liaising with the head (and sometimes bursar). On occasion, s/he may be called upon to take important decisions on behalf of the governing body between meetings. If there is a split vote, the chair usually has the casting vote. Above all, the chair must have the patience of a saint, drive and determination, and all the skills of a diplomat.

The chair should meet the head prior to every meeting at the school to ensure that they keep up-to-date with the school's business. S/he should also maintain close links with the vice-chair and chairs of the sub-committees.

In times of crisis, it may be that the chair will face the scrutiny of the media. They should take media training to ensure that s/he represents the school in a professional and discreet manner (see chapter on general information and guidance).

Overview of the chair's role:
- responsible for effective governance of the school;
- supports the head;
- chairs meetings of the governing body;
- ensures that the governing body keeps to the school development plan;
- oversees disciplinary proceedings and grievances, including ensuring governors stick to agreed processes;
- oversees allocation of governors to sub-committees;
- maintains close links with chairs of sub-committees;
- identifies prospective new governors and selects a mentor for the induction process (although the former role is increasingly delegated to a nominations committee);
- manages appointment of a new head and may sit in on interviews for new staff;
- appraises the head on her/his performance and leads the appraisal of awards for key staff;
- ensures that clear lines of responsibility are maintained between key school staff; and
- arranges their own succession.

The clerk
The clerk is responsible for the agenda. The post is often held by the bursar or school secretary (the latter at smaller schools). The clerk is responsible for convening meetings, agreeing dates for future meetings, taking and drafting minutes for approval at subsequent meetings, distributing minutes, and advising the governing body on procedural matters. The clerk, therefore, must be familiar with the school's governing documents and the laws affecting charitable independent schools. This post is usually a paid one.

If the clerk is also the bursar, it is imperative that the head's position is not undermined by governors seeking opinions independently of the head, through the clerk/bursar.

Meetings

Full governing body meetings should ideally take place every month of the school year, but at least once a term. Meetings should take no longer than an hour and a half and should stick to the agenda strictly, unless an unforeseen emergency has arisen. If meetings are allowed to drag on, some governors will lose their enthusiasm for the role.

Meetings should ideally be held at the school. If possible, they should be held during usual school hours to enable the governors to witness school life at first hand. This, however, may not be practical where governors hold full-time jobs and so may not be able to take time off.

The agenda should always contain:
- minutes of the previous meeting for sign-off by the governing body;
- head's report;
- financial report; and
- sub-committees' and working groups' reports.

These items should be sent with the agenda to all governors a week before a meeting to enable them to read and, if necessary, note queries to be raised at the meeting. Some governing bodies only receive these reports at the meeting, which makes it difficult for governors to query the information. Often, in this case, the head is unwilling to be challenged by governors: a cause for concern indeed.

Other items that should be periodically included in the agenda are:
- details of new laws or regulations that affect independent schools;
- educational reports and successes of pupils; and
- routine updates of the school's policies on, for example, bullying and special educational needs.

The head's report should contain indicators of how the school is performing against preset targets in the school development plan. It must be transparent so that governors can clearly identify strengths and weaknesses within the school. It should also indicate other matters, such as pastoral issues and staffing problems. In the latter instance, however, details should be kept to a minimum to avoid prejudicing subsequent disciplinary hearings.

Any other or private business should be tagged on to the end of a meeting. Requests from governors for items for inclusion under "any other business" should be sent to the clerk prior to the meeting. Sensitive matters, such as reviews of the head's or bursar's salary, should be held in private, without either of them present. The result of the private discussion should be announced afterwards to the affected party. Where the bursar is also the clerk and is under private discussion, the chair should note the outcome.

Minutes of meetings can be made available to parents on request or on the school website, with sensitive information withheld.

Sub-committees

Most governing bodies appoint a finance sub-committee (or finance and general purposes sub-committee, or finance and estates sub-committee) and a curriculum/education committee.

The finance sub-committee is responsible for recommending the school's annual budget and prospective fee increases for ratification by the full governing body. It reviews the school's expenditure against income, preferably on a termly basis to ensure that spending is kept on track. It also monitors the school's reserves and long-term investments, although these functions could even be carried out by a further specialist committee.

Where a proposed building work or other project is required that means that the school must borrow or embark on fundraising, the finance sub-committee will inform the full governing body of a decision and explain the general mechanics of the funding.

The finance sub-committee should be alert to overspending and/or shortfall in income and will recommend appropriate action. Apart from current financial performance, there are indicators for future success: pupil numbers now and in the future, pupil-staff ratios, total costs per pupil and the capital expenditure required to maintain and enhance standards.

The full governing body has the ultimate responsibility for these risks, but in practice delegates the responsibility to the finance sub-committee.

Timeline for financial planning:
- Autumn (half-term): sign off previous year's accounts and appoint auditors for next year/review previous year's financial performance;
- Spring: review and approve budget and set fees/review autumn term's financial performance; and
- Summer: confirm budget at half-term for new year/review spring term's financial performance.

The curriculum/education committee has a more supportive as opposed to assertive role, when compared to the finance sub-committee. It ensures that staffing and curricular changes are implemented. Some members of this sub-committee will occasionally observe lessons. Other sub-committees or working groups may develop other projects, such as fundraising.

With all sub-committees, it is essential that communication is maintained with the full governing body. Minutes for all sub-committees and working groups should be distributed prior to each meeting so that other governors have the opportunity to query and clarify the bases of decisions taken on their behalf.

Chapter **2**

The head's role; strategies and good practice for the appointment of a head and other academic appointments: by Susan Lawrence, Anita Bird and Bill Brown

For the purposes of this chapter, the term "governor" is used in a generic way to include both trustees and proprietors.

The headteacher provides the vision, leadership and direction for a school and ensures that it is managed and organised to meet the aims and targets set by the governing body. Her or his line manager is the chair of governors. The headteacher:

- is responsible for the internal organisation, management and control of the school, including leading and managing staff;
- advises on and implements the governing body's strategic framework and development;
- formulates aims and objectives, policies and targets for the governing body to consider formally adopting;
- formulates and implements policies to lead the school towards set targets;
- appraises or reviews performance, training, development and induction of staff;
- liaises with staff unions and associations;
- reports on progress to the governing body, ideally at least once a term, if not monthly;
- gives the governing body the necessary information to ensure that governors can assess that the headteacher's responsibilities and other delegated responsibilities have been fulfilled; and
- is accountable to the governing body for the school's performance in teaching, learning and pastoral care.

Heads need to be given the freedom to run the school in their own way, according to pre-agreed targets. While governors will measure their performance and success, it is important not to bog them down with intrusively burdensome scrutiny.

The head will keep the governing body informed with a detailed report at each governor meeting. It should provide details of everything from building plans to exclusions, so that governors are kept up-to-date with activities within the school.

The head will also often lead development (fundraising) at the school. Either directly or, if the school has a development director, as a campaign's public face. This can also encompass marketing eg for school open days.

A headteacher's leadership is critical to the success of a school. Although the school is run by a senior management team, the appointment of a head will always be the governing body's single most important responsibility. It is usual that a retiring head will announce their impending departure during the summer term before their last year, giving the governors a generous length of time to find a suitable successor. A younger, ambitious head may only be able to give a term's notice.

Autonomy is given to the headteacher in the appointment of staff. The involvement of the governors in this process varies from school to school, depending on the relationship between the governing body (whatever form this takes) and the headteacher. There must be clarity throughout over the powers of all parties, including the headteacher.

All schools should recognise that their most valuable resource is their staff. Whether appointing any member of staff, from headteacher to site worker, the school should be committed to ensuring that the candidate who best fits the post is appointed through informed and fair decision-making. The process should be taken seriously by all those involved and should be scrupulously fair. A school is a community: recruitment should involve as many of the stakeholders as possible to engender a sense of belonging and ownership that can underpin the school's ethos.

It is important that each stage of recruitment is well documented. Documentation will provide the necessary evidence should a decision be challenged or need justification. All evidence should be stored for an agreed length of time – at least six months (preferably 12 months). It is also worth noting that, under data protection law, candidates can access their interview notes, shortlisting information and any other documentation. Records, therefore, should be clear, factual, accurate and objective.

The principles involved in recruiting a staff member are fundamentally the same for each post; however, recruitment is likely to differ, depending on the needs of the post.

When appointing a headteacher, bursar, deputy headteacher or other post, a school should provide training for any new governor panel member. This is especially important in the appointment of a headteacher, where the appointing governors must establish clear and fair criteria and process, taking advice as necessary. All governors involved in the recruitment of staff should undergo safeguarding training, with reference to the vetting and barring scheme (see chapter on general information and guidance).

For any other staff members, schools should ensure that those interviewing and assessing candidates have received adequate training and are fully briefed on the process, the criteria to be used and their role. Usually this is undertaken by the headteacher or other senior member of staff.

Process
When a new or replacement post is being contemplated, the following

should be considered prior to any recruitment:

- why is the post needed?
- will the post be an additional headcount or will the existing structure need to be reorganised to meet the needs of the post?
- are there existing staff members who could fulfil the role, or is it likely to be an external appointment? and
- can the staffing budget accommodate the post?

Having addressed the above questions, the next step is to ensure that the job description has been drafted or, if it already exists, reviewed to reflect the current needs of the school. This job description will form the basis of the recruitment activity and is, therefore, critical. Time spent at this stage in refining the requirements and ensuring common understanding will save both time and resources, and will lead to a more successful appointment.

The job description should detail the post's specific duties and responsibilities. It is imperative that the job description is regularly reviewed as it will be used to assess performance and identify development needs.

For this purpose, all job descriptions should include:

- participation in the school's appraisal and/or performance management system, and in continuous professional development;
- active promotion of equal opportunities;
- compliance with data protection; and
- compliance with all school policies.

In addition, the following statement is highly recommended: "This job description is as it is at present – it is the practice of the school to periodically examine employees' roles and update them as necessary. This procedure is jointly conducted by the headteacher and line manager, overseen by a representative from the governing body in consultation with the employee. This could result in changes to the job description."

Hand-in-hand with the job description goes the person specification. The duties and responsibilities outlined in the job description determine the qualifications, relevant experience and skills required of a candidate to be successful in the post.

A clear person specification helps potential candidates to determine whether they are suitable for the role, and provides the basis for shortlisting and assessing applications for the position.

A clear person specification should cover the qualifications, experience, skills, knowledge and other requirements. It is helpful to separate the essential requirements from the desirable. When determining the requirements, it is advisable to review current equal opportunities legislation. For example, requiring a candidate to have ten years' experience discriminates against a younger candidate and, in any event, years of experience can be a blunt measure. Ten years' experience in a non-challenging environment can be less valuable than three years' experience in an educationally dynamic school. See example Person Specification Form and Shortlisting Criteria Form (Appendices 4 and 5).

To manage recruitment efficiently and effectively, the person leading the process should prepare a recruitment schedule. This should typically contain timings and actions and should identify those responsible for carrying out the actions. The actions might include:

- completion of the Staff Recruitment Form (see Appendix 1);
- posting the advertisement internally;
- deciding on the most appropriate external advertising media – this could include online as well as the printed press;
- collating an application pack, which should include job description, person specification, information sheet, prospectus, application form and medical questionnaire;
- briefing recruitment consultancies, if appropriate , and negotiating terms;
- setting up a Recruitment Tracking Form (see Appendix 2), which consists of a list of names of all who request details, where the advert was seen, and details of ethnicity and gender to help equal opportunities monitoring;
- collating the received applications;
- deciding on the selection steps, including interviews, presentations, written tasks, skills tests etc; and
- putting in place any practical, domestic arrangements.

Advertisement

When placing an advertisement, consider the most relevant publication (possibly the Times Educational Supplement: **www.tes.co.uk**) or website to your school, and also take into account the timing of publication. For example, many employers avoid advertising over a Bank Holiday weekend as candidates are less likely to respond. With the printed press, there is often the opportunity to take a second identical advert at a considerable discount; this is often to be recommended. However, where a newspaper is part of a larger group, sometimes it is not relevant to advertise in sister publications as the catchment area is often not appropriate.

The advantage of online advertising is that the advertisement is available to view for a longer period, typically one month. However, be clear about the closing date for your applications to avoid candidate applications arriving after the deadline. Where there is the facility to refresh the vacancy every week, this should be taken because this keeps your vacancy at the top of the listings.

When preparing an advertisement, consideration should be given to ensuring that:

- it attracts the attention of the intended audience;
- it retains interest; and
- it encourages response.

It is often helpful to have a standard template, as this will reflect the character of the school and is likely to be more cost-effective.

The narrative should contain:
- the title of the post;
- hours;
- salary scale;
- main responsibilities; and
- short details of the department and the school.

The requirements for any previous experience or any specific qualifications should also be stated. A safeguarding statement must be included (for an example statement, see Appendix 3).

In general, it is helpful to have a carefully designed and worded advertisement to secure maximum impact.

Shortlisting

A shortlisting meeting for members of the interview panel should be called as soon as possible after the closing date.

The applications should be screened by using the essential criteria established in the person specification. The interview panel should only select candidates for interview that have met all the "essential" criteria. If those candidates meeting the essential criteria are too many to interview, then "desirable" criteria can be used. The use of a reserve list is inadvisable, as it tends to raise any overlooked problems with the selection procedure.

Shortlisting decisions need to be recorded accurately so that they can be justified or challenged. When shortlisting, it is useful for the panel to consider:
- application form: is it clearly understood? Legible? Spelt and laid out correctly?
- employment history: what posts have they held? Why did they leave? How long in post? Any relevant training while in these posts?
- gaps in employment: have they been explained? If not, pursue at interview;
- skills, experience, training and any other qualifications: which skills have been gained by the candidate? To what extent does the breadth of experience of the candidate affect the strength of their application?
- attention to detail: did the candidate address the points asked for? Is there a personal or standard response and, if necessary, should this be probed further? and
- relevance: has the candidate related skills and experience to the

requirements of the post? Can they demonstrate that they have read all the information provided?

Once the shortlist of candidates has been agreed, then candidates will be invited for interview. References are requested. Unsuccessful candidates are informed by letter at this point.

As a guide, you should endeavour to inform candidates at least a week before interview. Interviews should be conducted approximately two weeks after the closing date (see Appendices 6 and 7 for Reference Request and Internal Appointments Forms).

Interview

The headteacher and/or chair of governors (or their delegated representatives) will provide guidance to interviewers at a pre-interview briefing, held to discuss procedure and lines of questioning. This guidance is essential as inexperienced interviewers can sometimes lack confidence, consistency, and an ability to produce reliable assessments of the candidate. The guidance should be based on developing the skills to ascertain a candidate's ability to achieve desired results within the post in question.

Many schools, when seeking a headteacher, find it helpful to offer potential interviewers the opportunity to take part in a mock interview. This provides them with a forum to test their questioning and assessment abilities, with the advantage that they can receive feedback from the "candidate".

Those chairing interview panels need to ensure that each panel member knows who will lead the questioning for each area, and will provide guidance on where to probe further into a response. S/he must also ensure that each panel member records their responses on the documents provided. It is recommended that staff and pupils meeting the candidates in a more informal capacity are also asked for their responses in writing.

The interview panel needs to be skilled in enabling the candidate to remain focused when answering questions. Usually, interviewers should ask open questions: why, where etc, but if a candidate is proving more expansive in their answers than was anticipated, some careful closed questions may be appropriate.

The chair has a crucial role in ensuring that the interview is genuinely two-way; candidates need to leave the interview with a favourable impression of the school, even if ultimately they are not selected.

As part of this, candidates must feel that the interview has been fair. A poorly carried out interview can leave a candidate feeling demoralised or that discrimination has taken place. The chair should ensure a universally high level of interest across all the candidates. Furthermore, the chair should ensure that heavy emphasis is placed on obtaining evidence to support any decisions that may be made following the interview stage. This will further help to deflect any accusations of discrimination made by candidates.

If a pupil panel is sitting, prior guidance discussion is essential so that a wide variety of areas is covered, although experience shows that pupils are very astute when judging people.

When candidates are asked to give a presentation, criteria for assessment needs to be discussed beforehand (eg you may prefer to do this without visual aids, ICT etc since part of the criteria should be to engage with an audience and use communication skills).

Other methods of assessment may be used in combination with an interview to assess the candidate's ability to function in the post. These may include:
- written exercises (to assess written communication skills and understanding of the application of knowledge);
- psychometric testing (to gain a greater understanding of a person's natural behavioural characteristics);
- aptitude/ability tests (to test for ability to deal with particular situations that may arise); and
- in-tray exercises (to allow the candidate to demonstrate how they might deal with, and order in importance, a list of urgent jobs).

If a lesson is to be observed, all interviewers should be familiar with the criteria for lesson observation assessment, similar to that used by the Independent Schools Inspectorate or Ofsted 162A.

Suitable accommodation for interviews should be arranged beforehand, eg seating arrangements; ensure a clock is visible; provide water; switch off mobile phones and divert telephone etc.

It is vital that an interview is conducted in a professional manner. The appointment of a competent chair to each panel is crucial. They will ensure that the interview is fair and structured by:
- welcoming the candidate, allowing the other members of the panel to introduce themselves and leading the interview;
- ensuring equal opportunities principles are followed;
- inviting the candidates to ask questions or to make any further comments in support of their application; and
- closing the interview and clearly outlining what happens next.

The panel should:
- be interested and attentive;
- avoid personal questions;
- avoid making moral judgements that may have a detrimental effect on its ability to assess the candidate reliably; and
- include "open" questions to create the opportunity for candidates to expand.

Open questions are ones that allow an extrapolation of a shorter answer. They allow the candidate to back up, or give examples of why they gave the response that they did. Examples of open questions that panel members might use are:

- from your experience, what has influenced your leadership style?
- what leadership initiatives have you introduced in your current role? and
- can you describe a time when you have developed a strategy or vision for an aspect of the school's development or improvement and how did you carry this strategy forwards?

Closed questions are ones that only allow for a "yes" or "no" response. These are usually best avoided, unless you wish to seek an affirmative response to a question that has been answered in an unclear or indistinct manner. Examples of closed question are:

- have you completed National Professional Qualification for Headship (NPQH) training?
- if the candidate's answer is no, ask: are you undertaking NPQH training? and
- if that answer is no, ask: if appointed, would you be willing to undertake NPQH training?

Probing questions may be used to yield information about a candidate that s/he originally forgot or did not include in an answer to a question. They can help to reveal the part that the candidate actually played in the resolution of a problem. They are also used to elaborate further on answers that were originally acquired from an open question. Examples are:

- what were your responsibilities?
- did you find that a helpful strategy to instigate? and
- would you repeat the route you took in dealing with that situation?

All interviewers should take notes (Appendix 8 provides example grids and forms used during the interview).

Post-interview

Interviewers should reserve judgement on individuals until the process is completed for all candidates. A meeting of all interviewers should be called to facilitate plenary and debate. It is advisable to hold the meeting immediately after the interviews. Some schools find it helpful to ensure that all the candidates remain available for further questioning or probing, should that be necessary. This is not always possible or even desirable, in which case candidates should be advised in advance of the interviews that they may be recalled or even telephoned at a later date for clarification.

Each individual should be asked in turn about each candidate. It is probably better to begin with less experienced members so that they will not feel influenced by others.

Evidence should be gathered, remembering that the candidates are being assessed not only against each other but, more importantly, against the requirements of the role. The interview panel will also want to take into account the candidates' levels of enthusiasm for the role and their motivation and commitment to the ethos of the school.

It is best to gain the consensus of all the interviewers on the choice of the successful candidate and great care should be taken if a majority view is going to be accepted. The reasons for the appointment should be recorded as should the reasons for rejecting the unsuccessful candidates. All paperwork that was generated from the interviews must be carefully filed so that only those persons with special permission are able to gain access to them.

Occasionally, an interview panel will decide to adapt the responsibilities of a post to make best use of the skills of an exceptional candidate, thus enhancing the quality of the post to the benefit of the school. In this situation, the job description should be revised and discussed with the preferred candidate prior to offer.

Once a decision has been made, the successful candidate should be offered the post verbally. It is important to remember that a binding contract of employment is made in this verbal offer. Unsuccessful candidates will be informed once the successful candidate has accepted. All candidates should be offered a debrief.

On verbal acceptance of the offer by the candidate, the conditional offer should be put in writing. This offer letter should clearly state that it is subject to contract and is conditional upon such areas as medical, CRB, qualification and identity checks being successfully completed. It is essential that the employer obtains the information required for the school's Central Register in order to enter the details onto the school's Single Central Record. The letter will also outline the main terms and conditions of employment, salary, major benefits and anticipated start date.

Only on notification of clear checks should the contract of employment be issued. The National College for Leadership of Schools and Children's Services currently recommends seeking this information prior to an interview: this could be time-consuming, though, if a large number of candidates is shortlisted.

Prior to the new staff member starting, the content of the induction process should be considered and tailored to the needs of the staff member, along with the timescale for completion.

If in doubt – do not appoint! Remember, all children deserve the best we can offer. If a mistake is made or a hasty and wrong decision is taken, it can take a great deal of time and effort to unravel. It is better to re-advertise and begin the process again to ensure the best fit.

The right approach

Sample questions for prospective heads:

General:
- what attracts you to the headship of this school?

Leadership:
- what strategies have proved useful in ensuring that a school is managed in the most effective and economic way to secure its long-term future?
- what has influenced your leadership style?
- what leadership initiatives have you personally introduced in your current role?
- which ones have had a beneficial impact on standards? and
- continuous development is essential in a highly effective school. How have you successfully managed resistance to change?

Strategic vision:
- a head must be able to formulate a vision or strategic plan for the school and have the ability to see it brought to fruition. Can you describe a time when you have developed a strategy or vision for an aspect of a school's development or improvement?
- how did you carry this strategy forwards?
- how did you get commitment from others to your strategy?
- what is your understanding of the school's ethos and how would you go about not only sustaining it but enhancing it? and
- tell us about those occasions when initiatives have proved less than successful, and how associated issues were overcome.

Business development:
- what have you found to be the key points in ensuring that a school is successful as an educational business and how have you achieved this success? and
- what actions would you take to maintain a balanced budget?

Duty of care:
- headteachers and proprietors are increasingly subject to litigation in areas concerning the discipline of children, complaints procedures, the competence of staff, curriculum provision, and health and safety. From your experience, what have you found useful in protecting the interests of your colleagues/proprietors?
- the ability for the school to thrive is dependent on a strong cashflow, which in turn has implications for ensuring the school is always full to capacity. How are you going to ensure that there is the maximum number of children on roll?
- what strategies have you used to ensure that there is a waiting list? and
- what personal experience have you had in identifying and developing alternative sources of finance?

General:
- the day-to-day life of a headteacher involves making many decisions. From your experience, how do you make decisions?

Strategic development:
- what sort of analytical processes have you used to help you take a strategic view of a school? and
- what principles and practices should a school pursue to secure the educational development of all of its pupils?

Teaching and learning:
- in this school, we are fortunate to have a significant number of able and talented pupils. Tell us what specific whole-school initiatives you have led to ensure that these pupils will benefit from a rich and challenging experience.
- how does a school best ensure that all children's special educational needs are met?
- in your experience, what action has been necessary to ensure that a school is compliant with the Special Education Need and Disability Act (SENDA)?
- tell us specifically how you have been involved in ensuring that teaching standards are consistently improved.
- tell us what experience you have had in pupil assessment.
- what are the key features in a reporting system to parents?
- how do you ensure that all pupils make good progress in each key stage?
- can you tell us about your experience in developing strategies to enable students to be self-motivated learners?
- tell us about an instance when you have motivated an under-achieving pupil.
- what strategies have you found useful in combating specific learning difficulties? and
- meeting the needs of able and talented children often presents teachers with a real challenge. What experience do you have of ensuring that these children are provided with appropriate teaching and learning?

Community:
- from your experience, how have you ensured that a school is at the heart of its community?
- what methods have you used to ensure effective communications with parents and children?
- there are times when schools have facilities that are under-used. How have you tackled this issue to ensure that not only is usage increased, but that the profile of the school is enhanced in the community?
- in what ways did you develop your school's current status in the community?
- what did you see as the school's main contribution to the local

community? and

- what will the parent body be saying about you in the car park at the end of your first term at this school and at the end of years one and two?

Here follow appendices to help effective recruitment in your school.

Copies of these forms are available to print out at
www.fismagazine.co.uk/strategic/recruitment/recruitment_printouts.html

Staff Recruitment Form

Department:

Post title:

Grade: Proposed start date:

Is this a new post? Yes/No
If no, name of previous post holder:

Details of post

Temporary/permanent:
if temporary, please state end date:

Full-time/part-time:
if part-time, number of hours/days per week:

Full-year/term-time:
if term-time, how many weeks per year?

Reason for the appointment:

Any changes to the previous post?

Job description updated?: Yes/No

Person specification prepared?: Yes/No

Advert agreed including closing date?: Yes/No

Where advert is to be placed:

Proposed interview date:

APPENDIX 2
Recruitment Tracking Form

Position: ....

No.	Name	Info pack sent	Letter/CV received and date	Interview	Invite sent	Feedback given by	Successful letter sent	Forms completed

Safer Recruitment Statement:

Our school is committed to safeguarding children and promoting the welfare of children and expects all staff and volunteers to share this commitment. We will ensure that all our recruitment and selection practices reflect this commitment. All successful candidates will be subject to Criminal Records Bureau checks along with other relevant employment checks.

Person Specification Form

Post title: ....

Education/qualifications or relevant experience	Essential:
	Desirable:
Experience/training	Essential:
	Desirable:
Skills/ability/knowledge	Essential:
	Desirable:
Other requirements	Essential:
	Desirable:

APPENDIX 5

Shortlisting Criteria Form

Post title: ....

Education/qualifications or relevant experience:	**A** Essential	**B** Desirable
Experience/training:	**C** Essential	**D** Desirable
Skills:	**E** Essential	**F** Desirable
Other:	**G**	
	H	
	I	

Criteria A, C and E must be ticked for an applicant to be selected for interview.

Applicant	A	B	C	D	E	F	G	H	I	Total	Shortlist? Y/N

Date: ....

APPENDIX 6

Reference Request Form

Candidate: .... Post: ....

How long and in what capacity have you known the candidate?

....

Please confirm the candidate's dates of employment:

....

Please confirm the number of days and reasons for sickness the candidate has had in the past year:

....

Why did the candidate leave/or is leaving your employment?

....

Are there any past or pending disciplinary/capability procedures relating to the candidate? Yes/No

If yes, please clarify: ....

Are there concerns about the candidate's suitability to work with children? Yes/No

If yes, please clarify: ....

Would you re-employ the candidate? Yes/No

In your opinion, is the candidate suitable to undertake this post? Yes/No

To your knowledge, does the candidate have a criminal record? Yes/No

Job description criteria	Strongly agree	Agree	Disagree	Strongly disagree
The candidate has excellent professional knowledge				
The candidate has undertaken a broad range of professional development and can work positively within a team				
The candidate has established excellent and appropriate working relationships with pupils				
The candidate has excellent working relationships with colleagues				
The candidate has developed good working relationships with parents				
The candidate is able to exercise appropriate classroom control and management of pupil behaviour				
The candidate has taken part in a range of extracurricular activities				
The candidate's health, attendance and punctuality are excellent				
The candidate has the ability to work under pressure				
The candidate can be relied on to reinforce the school ethos and has a positive approach to situations				
The candidate is enthusiastic and has emotional and personal stability				
I would recommend the candidate for this post without reservation				

Please record any additional comments that you would like to make about this candidate on the reverse of this form.

Signed: .... Position: .... Date: ....

APPENDIX 7
Internal Appointments/staff reference

Name of applicant: ....

Post applied for: ....

Number of years in present post: ....

Professional competence:
Administrative and organisational experience:
Relationships and co-operation with colleagues:
Relationships and work with pupils:
Attitude and application to work:
Record of health, attendance and punctuality:
Any disciplinary action currently pending?
Comments on the suitability of the applicant against the job description and person specification:

Example of forms used by interview panels
(these can be modified according to the candidate):

Assistant headteacher: INTERVIEW PANEL 1

Duration: 20 minutes

Panel: headteacher, chair, governor, head of maths

Subject: leadership and management

Suggestions for areas to be covered:
- management of transition;
- data analysis;
- professional development;
- leading an initiative;
- leadership and management style and qualities;
- areas of strength regarding job description; and
- line management.

These suggestions should form the main part of the interview. If there is time, ask supplementary questions.

Assistant headteacher: INTERVIEW PANEL 2

Duration: 20 minutes

Panel: deputy headteacher, chair, governor, head of year

Subject: personal characteristics

Areas to be covered:
- work/life balance;
- time management;
- coping with pressure;
- dealing with confrontation;
- team dynamics; and
- delegation.

These suggestions should form the main part of the interview. If there is time, ask supplementary questions.

Assistant headteacher: INTERVIEW PANEL 3

Duration: 20 minutes

Panel: deputy headteacher, chair, governor, finance officer

Subject: behaviour management

Areas to be covered:
- inclusion/exclusion;
- rights and responsibilities – pupils and staff;
- leading training in classroom management;
- tracking pupil progress;
- behavioural strategies; and
- assertive/positive discipline.

These suggestions should form the main part of the interview. If there is time, ask supplementary questions.

Assistant headteacher: INTERVIEW PANEL 4

Duration: 20 minutes

Panel: deputy headteacher, chair, governor, senior administration officer

Subject: teaching and learning

Areas to be covered:
- pupils with special needs;
- 14-19 curriculum;
- individualised/personalised learning;
- accelerated learning/gifted and talented pupils;
- educational pathways;
- monitoring and reporting progress; and
- performance management.

These suggestions should form the main part of the interview. If there is time, ask supplementary questions.

Presentation

Candidate: .... Panel member: ....

Scoring: 4 = criteria exceeded; 3 = criteria met; 2 = criteria partially met; 1 = criteria not met

10 minutes, without use of visual aids.

Topic	Comments	Score
Introduction: Did they introduce self; topic? Could I ask questions?		
Main body: Did it cover the topic asked for? Was it logical? Understandable? Interesting?		
Conclusion: Summarised main points? End on a positive note?		
General points: Keep to time? Vary the pace to keep me interested? Engage with the audience? Clear, concise communication?		

Total overall mark for the presentation ....

Overall comments: ....

....

....

Chapter **3**

The relationship between the governing body and
the head, and resolving disputes between them:
by Penny Chapman and Anita Bird

A key feature of a well-run school is a harmonious relationship between the
governing body and the headteacher. In this, a school is no different to any
charity or commercial organisation in which the governing body and chief
executive work in partnership; each knowing their roles and responsibilities
and respecting and supporting each other in the performance of them, which
is critical to the success of the organisation. Following the appointment
of a new headteacher, governors can feel that their key responsibilities to
the practical running of the school have been discharged but, in fact, the
responsibility of growing and maintaining the standards of the school,
through the auspices of the head, requires ongoing and careful attention.

The foundations of good performance

The governors of a (registered charity) school are the charity trustees, as
defined by the Charities Act 1993. The governors therefore have a statutory
responsibility for delivering the educational objects of the charity, yet the
head has the day-to-day task of running the school: as a result, there is an
almost inbuilt tension between them.

The head may resent the fact that although s/he has years of professional
experience of how the school should operate, s/he is accountable to a
group of governors, many of whom may have almost none. However, if the
governors are clear from the outset about their strategy for the school and
what they are looking for when appointing a head, the tensions should be
minimised and issues of underperformance are rare or, at least, capable of
being dealt with swiftly.

The school's constitution should permit the governors to delegate to the
head, the bursar and other members of senior staff, sufficient powers to
allow them to perform their roles. The terms of the delegated authority
should be clearly set out in the charity's bylaws, standing orders or other
policy documents.

The governors should regularly review how those powers have been
exercised and hold the head to account, according to the delegated authority.
It is advisable for one of the governors to take particular responsibility for
the relationship with the head. That person may be the chair, but must be
a governor with relevant skills whom the head respects as understanding
her/his role; who will act as her/his mentor and ensure that they feel fully
supported (although the governing body as a whole must guard against
the relationship becoming too cosy, such that the mentor is unable to be

objective about performance issues).

While the formal governance of a privately owned school may differ from that of a school established as or by a charity, of which the legal owners are the charity trustees, the fundamental principles for good management remain the same. Proprietors of a privately owned school may choose to set up an advisory board to help guide the school's progress, consisting of those skilled in education, finance, personnel, child welfare etc. While the proprietor will always retain the ultimate decision-making authority and legal responsibility for the school, the proprietor can delegate to the advisory board many of the roles that would generally be carried out by the board of trustees of a school owned by a charity, who are usually referred to as the governing body. If such an advisory board is established, it is particularly important for the responsibilities of the advisory board, the proprietor and the headteacher to be clearly laid out, so that each understands the role that they and others have with regard to the management and performance of the school so that the school can benefit from the co-ordinated expertise of all. However, the headteacher must be clear that s/he is employed by and answerable to the proprietor and not to the advisory board.

Establishing a good working relationship between the headteacher and the proprietor should be a priority for both parties; a shrewd proprietor will be able to judge whether s/he is best placed to take the role of mentor to the headteacher, or whether another person has more appropriate skills and experience. In either case, it is important that the headteacher understands the roles of all parties regarding the management and performance of the school.

In the rest of this chapter, governing body/governors is used to denote the legal owners of the school and not an advisory body.

Induction

The head must be clear from the time of appointment exactly what is expected of her/him, and it is important that the performance management system is implemented from the outset and not only when problems first arise.

When appointing a new head, governors should compile an induction pack that includes a copy of:
- the school's constitution;
- the governors' strategic objectives for the school;
- the policy documents that set out the relationship between the governors and the head, including lines and frequency of reporting, expected attendance at governors' meetings etc;
- the performance management system; and
- the disciplinary procedure.

However, the key to an effective induction is that the information provided is explained and discussed. When starting in a new role, many employees are deluged with "important" paperwork, which they promise themselves that they will read at a later date. Headteachers are no different in this regard. It is worth the time and effort on the governing body's part to talk the head through the documentation, and also the spirit and culture of the school. Of course, governors would expect that a new head will bring a fresh approach to some issues, but it is important that the head quickly understands the full context in which s/he is working, so that s/he can make sound judgements and start off on the right foot.

This induction should take place within a week of the head's joining the school, or ideally before s/he starts. At this time, the head and the governors should agree some short-term objectives so that the tone is set for the working relationship and that both parties are clear about the immediate measures of success.

Performance management systems
The head should be formally appraised at least once a year by a sub-committee of governors, chosen for their relevant skills, to be responsible for performance issues. At each appraisal, the governors should:
- review the achievement of previous objectives and understand the reasons for any non-performance;
- set clear objectives for the head for the forthcoming year;
- identify training and development needs;
- raise any areas of concern; and
- agree with the head a mechanism for following up any points arising out of the appraisal: this should then, in its turn, be monitored.

This appraisal should be formally documented, with copies for the head, the governor-mentor, and for the head's personnel file, which should not be kept with other HR records.

It is vital that appraisal is an ongoing process, not just a once-a-year activity. The governor-mentor should meet the head regularly to discuss her/his progress against the objectives set. This provides an opportunity for informal feedback for the head, not only on what s/he is doing but, equally importantly, on the way in which s/he is doing it. The governor-mentor should see themselves as a "critical friend", in a supporting role, but always with professional distance maintained. It is prudent for the governor-mentor to make contemporaneous notes of these meetings so that, if difficulties do arise, the school has evidence of the issues that were raised.

Early warning signs of poor performance
The performance management tools, mentoring systems and review mechanisms ought to provide an early warning system to the governors if

the head is underperforming. If, for example, the quality of the head's reports diminishes, or becomes less detailed, then it may be a sign that the head is not getting to grips with, or has lost her/his grip, on the management of the school.

Other early warning signs:
- staff complaints;
- concerns raised by the bursar over financial irregularities;
- an increase in parent complaints or falling off of roll numbers;
- secrecy or lack of willingness to share information; and
- resentment of the mentor's role.

The governors will only benefit from these early warning signs if mechanisms are in place for individuals other than the head to communicate directly with the governors. For example, a governor with financial skills ought to have regular one-on-one review meetings with the bursar, another governor should attend occasional staff meetings and, once a year, the governors should consider holding an open forum for parents.

What if underperformance begins to damage the school?

The key is to be prepared. Underperformance by the head needs swift, active management, which will need to take place outside the context of the governors' regular meetings; partly because the governors are unlikely to meet frequently enough to deal with the matter, partly because the head will usually be in attendance at the governors' meetings and partly to minimise the spread of knowledge of the underperformance unless and until necessary. The members of the sub-committee responsible for performance issues should convene to take control of the situation as soon as they realise there is a potentially serious problem.

The governors will need to consider whether:
- the underperformance is an appraisal issue that needs training or other assistance;
- it is a disciplinary matter requiring the disciplinary procedure to be invoked. If it is or may be, the school's external legal advisors should be asked to advise on the employment law position at the earliest possible opportunity to minimise any claim which the head might subsequently make; or
- if it is, potentially, a criminal offence: for example, in a worst case scenario, child abuse, which might need to involve the police. In these circumstances, in addition to the relevant employment/criminal law, the governors must consider reputational issues. It is important to have a pre-prepared communication strategy to invoke in such circumstances and that the governors accept cabinet responsibility in dealing with the matter.

If the underperformance is a general failure to achieve the objectives and targets set by the governors, despite appropriate training and support, it is important that the disciplinary procedures are carefully followed and the head is given the opportunity to improve and to learn from mistakes. If a head is not proving to be successful, the governors should also consider whether they not only need to review the performance of the head, but also the basis on which they have delegated their powers and their own performance in properly monitoring that delegation.

However, if the underperformance persists and the disciplinary procedures have been exhausted, the governors must protect the interests of the school and of its pupils by dismissing the head. Handling the exit of an underperforming head is not easy, but if robust performance management systems are in place from the outset and the correct disciplinary procedures have been followed, the governors should be able to remove the head with the minimum of reputational risk to the school.

Occasionally, situations arise when it would be damaging to the school to leave an underperforming head in post during a performance management process that is likely to be lengthy. The governors may feel that the head needs to be removed quickly. Such decisions should not be reached lightly as they could have serious reputational repercussions for the school; a school that promotes a caring environment for staff and parents could be seen as acting counter-culturally by dismissing a head in a way that is seen to be harsh.

The governors of a charitable trust school must be particularly careful as they are under an obligation to spend the charity's money for the purpose for which it was intended, which generally does not include large pay-offs to compensate for unfair dismissal.

Nevertheless, there are occasions when, having taken all aspects into consideration, the governors decide that the immediate removal of the head is the only course of action. At this point, it is imperative that legal advice is sought and followed as failure to do so can have a high financial cost to the school. The likely result is that the governors will approach the head to explain their concerns and to offer a compromise agreement: this is a formal legal agreement between the school and the head where, in exchange for a sum of money to compensate the head for the loss of her/his position, s/he undertakes not to bring proceedings against the school. In addition, agreements covering confidentiality, the giving of a reference and statements to parents are often included.

Other parties too

Governors should be aware that the head would usually involve her/his union in the financial negotiations, and it is not unusual for a school to have to pay a sum equivalent to one year's gross salary. However, no number of policies and procedures can be a substitute for a genuine working partnership between the governors and the head in which each have clearly defined roles and respect for each other, so that matters of concern can be openly addressed at an early stage to minimise the opportunity for underperformance to escalate to the point where it may have a negative effect on the success of the school.

Chapter **4**

The bursar and finance: the bursar's responsibilities, financial control and financial viability: by Tracey Young and David Sewell

The role of the bursar varies substantially from school to school, depending on the specific needs of the governing body and the nature of the school. The bursar will typically have operational responsibility for all of the school's non-educational activities, with education and pastoral care usually being the direct responsibility of the head. If the head can be seen as the school's chief executive, the bursar is its finance director and head of administration.

The bursar's responsibilities, therefore, include the following broad areas:
- finance;
- premises/facilities;
- support staff; and
- liaison with the community and with the school's advisors.

In larger schools, the bursar may have a number of subordinates with narrower responsibilities (such as finance bursar and property/estates bursar), but the ultimate responsibility will rest with the bursar. The role of bursar is often, although not always, combined with that of clerk to the governing body. Whether or not the bursar is also the clerk, liaising with the governing body and any relevant sub-committees is a key part of the bursar's role.

The bursar is usually appointed by the governors and has a reporting line to the governing body as well as the head.

Finance
Financial management and financial reporting are key responsibilities that are common to the bursars of every school. The bursar does not need to hold formal financial or accounting qualifications if someone in her/his finance team has this expertise, but they need to be comfortable with financial information and reporting. As a general rule, the smaller the school, the more hands-on the bursar will need to be.

The bursar will be responsible for ensuring that the school's annual accounts are compliant with reporting requirements and current best practice within the independent schools sector. For schools that are incorporated under the Companies Act, the bursar may also be the company secretary.

Key responsibilities within the finance function include:
- budgeting and monitoring of performance;
- proposing fee levels;
- administration of bursaries and scholarships;
- billing and debt collection;

- monitoring and operation of financial controls;
- processing accounting information;
- administration of payroll, pensions and purchase ledger;
- preparation of management accounts and statutory financial statements;
- liaison with the external auditors;
- compliance with statutory filing requirements; and
- administration of non-charitable trading (shop, summer lettings etc).

Premises/facilities management

Premises or estates management is one of the more variable roles of the bursar. In a small urban day school, premises management may amount to little more than routine maintenance and cleaning of the school building. A large rural boarding school may have substantial building projects as well as grounds to maintain, over and above the upkeep of the school buildings.

Key responsibilities within premises management include:
- monitoring of routine maintenance work and upkeep of the school grounds;
- management of refurbishment and major building projects;
- compliance with regulations: fire safety, health and safety etc;
- management of the school's IT infrastructure; and
- lettings and other external use of school facilities.

Support staff

Teaching staff will usually be the direct responsibility of the head, supported by the HR department, where applicable. The HR function itself, including recruitment, appraisal and disciplinary procedures for all support staff, would usually fall under the bursar's responsibility. The registrar, marketing, fundraising and alumni departments are often the responsibility of the head. However, the scope and allocation of these responsibilities will vary from school to school.

Support staff would typically include these functions:
- maintenance/grounds;
- catering and cleaning (including outsourcing arrangements);
- school shop; and
- administration.

External liaison

Liaison with the local community is becoming even more important for schools as they address the requirements of the public benefit test brought in by the Charities Act 2006. Making best use of the school's facilities from a financial point of view (eg summer lets and private events) has always been within the bursar's remit. The new public benefit requirements add a new dimension to this role: although the Charity Commission's view from test cases has been focused on provision of bursaries, this may in time be broadened to include sharing facilities with the maintained sector.

The bursar's role is wide-ranging (and often includes the role of clerk to the governors), but the chief responsibility is for the school's finances, in particular the monitoring of financial performance and the operation of financial controls. The bursar is also a key source of information, both financial and operational, for the governors to assist them in making decisions for the furtherance of the school's objects and the safeguarding of its assets.

Financial control responsibilities of governors

As a governor, you are, along with the other members of the governing body, responsible for the control and management of your school. This means that you must ensure that the school remains solvent, is well run, complies with all obligations and that funds and assets are used reasonably in line with its objects. Your tenure is likely to be a very short period in the overall life of the school, so you must remember that you are a guardian of the school assets not just for current but future generations too.

One of your key responsibilities is ensuring financial control. As with any organisation, good financial management is imperative to success and to secure the long-term future of the school. Detailed below are the main areas to consider in financial control.

Internal controls

Governors should maintain and regularly review the school's internal controls, reporting, policies and procedures. Generally, governors will delegate day-to-day running of the school to management, but this does not remove your responsibilities to protect the school's assets. This means that the head and bursar will often operate the internal controls, but governors must ensure the necessary controls are in place and that they are being operated correctly.

A brief summary of key internal controls (to be set in one document called "Financial regulations") include:

- segregation of duties ensures that one person does not record and process a complete transaction. This reduces the likelihood of errors and deliberate manipulation. In many schools with a small bursary department, the ability to segregate duties can be limited. However, involvement of the head in financial processes can ensure appropriate authorisation of transactions. In some cases, involvement of governors will be necessary;
- all purchases should be authorised before they are ordered and all supporting documentation should be retained. Clear and documented authorisation limits should be applied. Significant purchases should be authorised by governors. Payments should only be made on the receipt

of an original invoice that has a purchase order and a delivery note;

- cheque payments should require two signatures. Cheque signatories should generally include the bursar, head and a selection of governors. For cheques above a specified level, say £5,000, a governor's signature should be required. Cheques should only be signed on a review of the documentation to support the payment;
- electronic payments should follow the same approval procedures as cheque payments. Two individuals should be required to approve a payment and, when payments are above a certain limit, governor approval should be necessary;
- cash payments should be avoided, where possible. Any cash held onsite should be kept to a minimum. Cash should be kept securely, with limited access. Petty cash should be operated on an imprest system, with supporting documentation obtained for all cash payments; and
- salaries are a significant expense for schools, so strong controls are essential. All staff appointments should be authorised by the governors, with employment contracts in place. Salaries should be authorised and documented. The payroll should be prepared and reviewed by different individuals to ensure that errors have not been made and that fictitious employees are not included. Salary payments should not be made by the individual who has prepared the payroll, unless a second authorisation is required.

Governors should have a system of regular review to ensure that internal controls are operating effectively. In some cases, it may be advisable to have an internal audit.

Fixed assets

Fixed assets are buildings, fixtures and fittings, books and equipment, computers and motor vehicles. It is recommended that a register of fixed assets is maintained. A regular check should be made to ensure that they are in good repair and to ensure they remain in use by the school. This will ensure that any misappropriation of assets is identified and can be challenged.

Fixed assets, in particular buildings, often represent a significant proportion of the assets of a school and without them the school would be unable to operate. It is therefore essential that such assets are adequately insured.

Investments

Some schools hold investments to generate income and to secure the capital. Governors have a duty to ensure these assets are safeguarded. The key controls to be observed for investments are that:

- the governing body should set an investment policy;
- professional advice should be sought when managing an investment portfolio. It is common for the management of a portfolio to be

delegated to an investment manager;
- it should be ensured that all dividends or interest are received promptly and all investment sales and purchases are authorised;
- the governing body should review the performance of the school's investments and the investment managers; and
- the investment portfolio should be diversified to limit risk.

Financial information

Governors are responsible for ensuring that the school keeps proper books and records. Up-to-date financial information (including termly management accounts, budgets and cashflow forecasts) is essential for the governing body to maintain good financial control.

The governing body is also responsible for preparing the financial statements of the school, in accordance with the Charities Act and the Statement of Recommended Practice (SORP). If the school is an incorporated charity, the accounts will also need to comply with the Companies Act.

The SORP requires the financial statements to include the following:
- governors' report;
- statement of financial activities (SOFA);
- balance sheet; and
- notes to the financial statements.

An example of an independent school accounts is included on the Charity Commission website (**www.charity-commission.gov.uk**).

The governors' report is written by the governors under the guidelines provided by the SORP. This provides the governors with an opportunity to explain to the readers of the accounts about the objects of the school, its aims, activities, achievements and future plans. It is not just a compliance document as it can be used to promote your school and its achievements. A summary of its information will also be included in the summary information return, Part C of the annual return to the Charity Commission.

Good financial control is essential to the smooth running of a school and to ensure that the assets are safeguarded. The governing body is ultimately responsible for the school and its assets. Ensuring procedures and controls are in place, and performing regular reviews to ensure they are being followed, will protect both the school and you as a governor.

Financial viability

It is essential that governors have a good understanding of the financial position of a school and take action appropriate to the state of the finances. Making the wrong financial decisions can have implications for the school, pupils and parents for years to come and could put the long-term viability of the school in jeopardy. As a governor, you have an opportunity to make a difference to a school with which you feel an affinity, perhaps because you were a pupil or your children attend or have attended the school, but it comes with a great responsibility and, sometimes, the need to make tough decisions. Ultimately, you have a duty to protect the assets of your school and must act prudently in administering its financial affairs.

Detailed below is information the governing body should have and consider on a regular basis to ensure it can make informed decisions.

Monitoring

The availability and monitoring of up-to-date and accurate information is crucial. The cash position, debt level, results and pupil numbers (both current and prospective, by year group) should be reviewed on a regular basis (usually once a term) and budgets and cashflow forecasts updated to reflect the revised position. This will enable action to be taken in a timely fashion, based on accurate information. In addition, consideration of key performance indicators and benchmarking against trends in similar schools should enable the school to identify issues and changes that can be made.

Planning

Preparation of realistic and reliable budgets and cashflow forecasts (looking three to five years' ahead) is essential. These should be updated with changes and actual figures during the year so that the school has a clear idea of its outturn for the year.

Actual results should be compared to the budget on a regular basis to identify significant variances so that they can be investigated, action taken and the forecast adjusted.

Sensitivity analysis

Performing a sensitivity analysis on budgets and cashflow forecasts is a useful tool in enabling a school to identify the impacts of changes in pupil numbers and major expenditure items on the results and cash levels. Longer-term forecasting illustrates the impact of reductions in rolls over a sustained period and the ripple effect this has in the future. Contingency planning for a worst-case scenario enables governors to consider what action they would need to take and the long-term viability of the school.

Capital and maintenance plans

It is important for a school to have well maintained and up-to-date facilities to enable it to remain competitive. Cutting spending on repairs and maintenance and delaying capital projects can help schools through cashflow difficulties, but cannot be continued indefinitely.

Prepare a costed rolling-maintenance programme and capital spending plan for five to ten years, which can be incorporated into the school's budgets and cashflow forecasts. This will give governors a clear idea of the costs they will need to incur and enable them to assess what action they may need to take to meet those costs.

Threats to pupil numbers

Knowledge of current and prospective pupil numbers, including potential threats, is essential in understanding the financial viability of your school and enabling you to plan effectively. Monitor the following areas:

- economic conditions: increases in unemployment and recession are likely to result in reductions in pupil numbers for many schools. In these circumstances, it is common for there to be a time lag in the impact on schools and they often feel the effects for longer;
- demographics: changes in birth rates and the age profile of your catchment area can have a significant impact on the number of potential pupils;
- competitors: keeping abreast of your competitors and what they offer is essential. This includes the state sector; and
- local businesses: if you have a significant number of pupils whose parents are employed by the same employer, consideration should be given to the risk of the business closing and the impact on the pupil roll.

Borrowings

Most schools undertake major projects to update old buildings or provide new facilities, often funded through loans. Governors must take special care when borrowing funds since they may be putting the school's assets at risk.

It is important to prepare detailed cashflow forecasts to ensure that the school is able to make loan repayments and perform a sensitivity analysis to assess the potential risk of not being able to meet the repayments. Consideration should also be given to major spending requirements in the future, which may not be possible because the school continues to make repayments for old projects. It may be appropriate to increase current fee levels to enable earlier repayment of a loan or fundraise to finance part or all of the project.

Making changes

When a school is in financial difficulties or anticipates experiencing difficulties in the future, it is important that informed decisions are taken quickly. Areas to consider are:

- the strategic direction of the school, covering areas such as:
  - becoming co-educational throughout or in part of the school;
  - increasing or decreasing age range of pupils. For example, opening a nursery or closing a sixth form where pupil numbers are insufficient;
  - offering or extending bus routes to increase the catchment area;
  - recruiting pupils from overseas;
  - closure of boarding facilities; and
  - reducing range of courses offered;
- careful review of the school's cost base, considering those costs that are fixed and those that are variable. Where continued deficits are made,

costs need to be reviewed in detail and cuts made; and
- fee increases may be required.

It must be remembered that, to make some of the above changes, Charity Commission agreement may have to be sought.

The final step

By being fully aware of the financial position of your school and having the opportunity to manage change effectively, a school in financial difficulties can survive. However, this is not always possible. In this situation, governors have a duty to ensure prudent financial management and compliance with the law, including insolvency law. They must, therefore, act swiftly and decisively to protect the interest of their pupils and the assets of the charity. Where a school is trading while insolvent, there can be serious consequences for the governors, which could result in personal liabilities (see chapter on governor liabilities).

When a school is unable to survive, the options available to governors are to merge the school with another or close.

Mergers and closures

A merger is often felt to be the best option, enabling the school to continue in a different form. It can provide a better continuity of education for pupils and enable retention of at least some of the school's staff. However, finding a suitable merger partner can be difficult. If the current governing body has been unable to make the school financially viable, then it may be unlikely that a new organisation will succeed, unless drastic changes are made. Where your school has insufficient net assets, another charity may be loath to risk their own.

Closure may be the only option, which can be an extremely painful process and requires a significant amount of governors' time. However, where the school has a valuable site that can be sold, the governors can in time use the funds to fulfil the objects of the charity in other ways. Depending on restrictions imposed by the objects of the charity, the funds could be used to fund bursaries for pupils in other schools or they can be gifted to a school with similar objects to support their activities.

To dispose of the school's assets, the governors should apply to the Charity Commission for permission. In practice, the commission will allow assets to be moved to a new entity or sold to pay off creditors.

Chapter **5**

Inspections: by Andrew Maiden

Inspections evaluate the effectiveness of schools. They also examine the abilities of the head and governing body (from policy documents, finances and development plans), and measure the quality of education and pastoral care provided to pupils (from results, pupils' work, balance of the curriculum and lesson observations). ISI inspections will also assess compliance with the Independent School Standards Regulations (ISSR) – a primary feature of the new inspection regime.

Inspections, although intended to give schools the opportunity to show themselves at their best, are inevitably stressful. Despite this pressure, it is important for governors to remain calm. If the school has followed sound governance procedures, then there should be little to worry about. In fact, most governing bodies should be proud of their school. However, they should guard against making exaggerated or false claims on the school's behalf; self-evaluation should be realistic and reasonable.

Inspectors are often serving or former heads, led by a registered inspector. The chair of governors and other key governors (such as the chair of finance) will be interviewed by the inspectors on governance and general oversight.

At the end of the inspection, the governing body is given an oral report by the lead inspector. This is an opportunity to correct factual inaccuracies in the draft report, but governors will not be able to alter the general conclusions.

It is important to be clear about which regulations apply to your school and to make sure that you are properly registered with the relevant registering authority. A central requirement for all independent schools is that they must be registered with the Department for Education (DfE) and so must adhere to the ISSR. If schools also have provision for under-3s, then they must also register for Early Years Foundation Stage (EYFS) with Ofsted. The EYFS requirements are applicable to all children under five years of age. In Independent Schools Council (ISC) schools, the inspection will report on compliance with both the ISSR and EYFS requirements. Schools with residential provision (boarding) must also meet the National Minimum Standards (NMS), now inspected by Ofsted (previously the Commission for Social Care Inspection). In addition to these education-based regulations, schools are subject to a number of other legal requirements, such as health and safety, and employment legislation.

The Independent Schools Inspectorate (ISI) inspects schools in England that are members of the ISC associations; for non-members of the ISC in England, inspections are carried out by Ofsted. In Scotland, the role is managed by HM Inspectorate of Education; in Northern Ireland, by the Education and Training Inspectorate; and in Wales by Estyn.

The final report is sent to the head, the school's member association (where appropriate), and the DfE. Two weeks later, the report must be sent to parents. The head will be asked to write to respond to their association and thence to ISI (copied to the DfE), setting out how the school will meet the report's recommendations. The letter should set out remedial action, a feasible timetable and criteria for implementation. The report will be published on the ISI website.

It is then incumbent on governors to ensure that any reported shortcomings or failings in the report are addressed in the subsequent months.

The specifics of different types of inspections are outlined below.

ISI inspections

The ISI is a not-for-profit organisation and is answerable to the DfE on whether ISC member schools meet their statutory requirements. It is monitored by Ofsted on behalf of the DfE.

Independent schools receive five days' notice of an inspection and will usually be inspected every three years. This, however, is regularly subject to change. Check the ISI website for latest guidance (**www.isi.net**). Inspection is in two forms: standard and interim.

ISI standard inspections

The ISI office notifies schools of an impending inspection. Five days later, a reporting inspector and a team inspector visit the school for two days. For schools with an EYFS provision, early years inspectors will also visit. The inspection reviews how well a school meets its regulatory requirements and includes, for example, scrutiny of documents as well as some lesson observation. Feedback on the school's compliance with regulations is given at the end of the visit, and the regulatory findings are reported to ISI and the DfE.

Four weeks later, the same reporting inspector returns to the school with a team of up to four inspectors per section of the school. They spend two and a half days in school, gathering additional evidence on the quality of provision and outcomes for children. They will also note improvements that the school may have made in response to possible earlier regulatory failings. Action taken by the school is recorded in the final report along with the record of compliance made at the initial visit.

ISI interim inspections

Interim inspections begin in the same way as standard inspections, but without the second visit four weeks later. They thus concentrate solely on compliance with Regulations.

Key features of ISI inspection teams:

- schools are inspected in accordance with how they are registered with the DfE. For example, a school with one registration for pupils aged 3-18 will be inspected as one event, even if previously the junior and senior sections have been inspected separately. If your school has separate registrations for different sections, then they will have separate inspections and reports, though inspection may still occur at the same time;
- reporting inspectors will be allocated for each school, as defined by association membership. Therefore, senior and junior schools in membership of different associations will each have an allocated reporting inspector;
- assistant reporting inspectors will be allocated for split sites, and for sections of all-age schools that have more than 400 pupils;
- specially trained EYFS inspectors are allocated for schools where there are pupils up to and including age 5; and
- for standard inspections, team sizes vary from between one and four team inspectors for each section of a school. Usually, inspection teams include an association head. Teams cover a range of curriculum areas to ensure that a good range of lessons are observed.

Once an inspection is notified, schools are asked to supply the reporting inspector with various documents and information, including, for example, up-to-date self-evaluation, a staff list, a timetable for the days when the reporting inspector will be in school, a plan of the school, the times of the school day and the policies required for compliance with regulations.

Parent and pupil questionnaires form an important part of both standard and interim inspections.

Costs
There is a standard annual fee (ranging between £500 and £8,000, depending on the type of school), with a sliding scale per pupil in schools with more than 150 pupils.

Other inspections
Schools in England that are not members of the ISC associations are inspected by Ofsted. In inspecting these schools, Ofsted uses the powers granted by section 162A of the Education Act 2005. For this reason, these inspections are sometimes known as "section 162A inspections".

Ofsted also inspects provision in these schools for children aged up to 5 against the Framework for the Early Years Foundation Stage.

The inspection of educational provision in non-association independent schools is generally carried out every three years. The results are published on Ofsted's website.

Ofsted also inspects the welfare (care) of boarders in independent schools, according to the National Minimum Standards and the Every Child Matters outcomes for children. Inspectors judge whether the school satisfies the regulations for registration and, where it does not, it is required by the DfE to produce an action plan for improvement. Failure to make the necessary improvement(s) may lead to the school being removed from the register of independent schools and may be required to close.

Similar work is carried out by HM Inspectorate of Education (in Scotland), by the Education and Training Inspectorate (in Northern Ireland) and by Estyn (in Wales).

The Bridge Schools Inspectorate (BSI) has approval from the Secretary of State for Education from September 2008 to inspect schools belonging to the Christian Schools' Trust and the Association of Muslim Schools throughout England.

BSI provides an opportunity for co-operation between faith groups to establish a specialist faith schools inspectorate that respects their distinctive ethos. Ofsted monitors the work of independent inspectorates, including a sample of reports.

Governor checklist
Governors should satisfy themselves that:
- the recommendations made at the last inspection have been addressed;
- the school has robust systems for checking compliance with Regulations;
- all necessary staff recruitment checks have been carried out and documented, and recorded in the central register of appointments;
- there are effective systems for reviewing and approving welfare and educational policies;
- the annual review of the school's arrangements for safeguarding pupils' welfare has been formally adopted and recorded in the minutes;
- the school's health and safety arrangements comply with regulations;
- the school's three-year disability access plan meets the requirements and contains appropriate timescales; and
- the school's complaints policy for parents includes all the required elements.

Legal checklist
- Education Act 2002 (Education (Independent School Standards) (England) Regulations 2003 as amended 2005, 2007, 2009;
- Childcare Act 2006 (Early Years Foundation Stage requirements);
- Children Act 1989 as amended by the Care Standards Act 2000 (National Minimum Standards (NMS) for Boarding Schools); and
- Other regulations and requirements: Special Educational Needs and Disability Act (SENDA), health and safety, employment legislation etc.

Chapter **6**

Governor liabilities: legal structures of independent schools, governors' duties to the school, general liabilities, Corporate Manslaughter Act, personal liability, insurance: by Barney Northover and Con Alexander

Charities that operate independent schools vary widely in their legal structures. It is the legal structure that determines how the charity is regulated and governed, and also the personal liabilities of those who direct or govern it.

Some schools are structured as corporations established by Royal Charter or special Act of Parliament; some are limited companies formed under the Companies Acts; and others are unincorporated associations or unincorporated trusts.

Incorporated charities in general
Charities can be incorporated as corporations, companies or as charitable incorporated organisations (CIOs). Corporations can be formed under a Royal Charter or by an Act of Parliament. Companies are formed under the Companies Acts. Additionally, it will be possible to form CIOs under the Charities Acts.

An incorporated charity has its own name and a corporate identity separate from that of its members. It is said to have its own legal personality and has perpetual succession. It will be the employer of the head, the bursar and all the staff and will be the contracting party with parents, the bank, professional advisers and other suppliers.

An incorporated charity can hold its general property beneficially, but cannot hold general property subject to restrictions as to how it can be liquidated and spent. It may accept specific property on charitable trusts, including permanent endowment trusts, in which case it acts as a corporate trustee.

Royal Charter corporations
The Sovereign has the power to incorporate a body by granting a Royal Charter. A body incorporated by Royal Charter has all the powers of a natural person, including the power to sue and be sued in its own right. Royal Charters were, at one time, the only means of incorporating a body, but there are now other means (becoming a registered company, for example), so the granting of new charters is comparatively rare and is generally confined to eminent professional bodies or charities that have a sustained record of achievement.

The charter sets out the objects of the corporation and the powers of the trustees in pursuing the objects. The affairs of the corporation are controlled by a body of trustees in accordance with bylaws set out in the schedule to the charter.

There is also a body of members who are sometimes the same individuals as the trustees, but need not be. The members of a corporation enjoy limited liability unless the charter or act creating it provides otherwise.

Special Acts of Parliament

A few schools are corporations constituted by a special Act of Parliament. The act usually specifies the objects and powers. The trustees are regulated by statutes, which are the equivalent of bylaws under a Royal Charter. Amendment of the statutes usually requires the approval of the Sovereign-in-Council.

Limited companies

Companies limited by guarantee are the most common legal structure for charities that operate independent schools. A limited company is, like a corporation, a legal person in its own right. It is said to have its own legal personality, separate from that of its members and directors.

Commercial companies will usually be limited by shares as a means of regulating voting rights and the distribution of profits. However, charitable companies are expected to take the form of a company limited by guarantee and are not required to, although may, include the word "limited" in the company's name.

Charitable companies have members and directors. Usually the members and directors of a charitable company limited by guarantee that operates an independent school will be the same individuals, but the function of directors is quite different to that of members.

In the case of a school, the directors are usually known as "governors" or "trustees". They are charity trustees within the meaning of the Charities Acts, being the people who are responsible for the running of the charity and the school.

The members have limited statutory powers which cannot be taken away from them, but which can only be exercised in a general meeting or in certain circumstances by written resolution. They are entitled to have an annual general meeting, consider the accounts, appoint the auditors, and appoint and remove directors. They also have power to amend the memorandum and articles of association, subject to the consent of the Charity Commission for the objects, certain powers, trustee benefit provisions and the dissolution clause.

The memorandum of association sets out the objects of the company and the powers of the directors in pursuing the objects. The articles of association regulate and set out the rights of the members and the directors.

Charitable incorporated organisations

A charitable incorporated organisation (CIO) is a new form of incorporated charity created in the Charities Act 2006. They are designed exclusively for charities and are intended to provide an incorporated structure that avoids regulation under the Companies Acts.

At the time of writing, the regulations relating to CIOs are still out for consultation, but in their draft form they largely resemble the regulations governing charitable companies limited by guarantee.

There is provision for existing charitable companies limited by guarantee to be able to convert to CIO status. However, many professional advisers urge caution as, with any new legal structure, there is likely to be teething trouble with the model and a risk that charities opting to become a CIO may become the defendant in a test case.

Unincorporated charities

An unincorporated charity may be governed by a trust deed or a Charity Commission scheme. It has no legal personality or entity and exists only by its trustees and its purposes.

Certificate of incorporation

For administrative efficiency, the trustees of an unincorporated charity can obtain a certificate of incorporation under Part VII of the Charities Act 1993, enabling them to sue and be sued and also to hold land under a general corporate name. A certificate does not, however, confer limited liability on the trustees or governors of a school.

Corporate trustee

The trustee of an unincorporated charity can itself be an incorporated body. A corporate trustee may be appointed by the Charity Commission or pursuant to powers in the charity's governing instrument.

A corporate trustee of an independent school charity is likely to have the governors as its directors and members, who will have limited liability in the same way as the governors of an incorporated charity. However, the corporate trustee is not itself a charity and the structure can be confusing for governors and third parties alike, because the objects and powers in the memorandum of association of the corporate trustee are not available to governors for charitable assets or activities. Where this is misunderstood, there is a risk of liabilities for governors who inadvertently act outside their powers.

There are also complications arising from the law relating to trust corporations and when considering the application of the Transfer of Undertakings (Protection of Employment) Regulations 2006 (TUPE).

Governors' duties

Regardless of how their charity is constituted, the people who serve on the governing body and are responsible for controlling the management and administration of the charity:

- are charity trustees within the meaning of s.97(1) of the Charities Act 1993;
- each have the same duties and responsibilities; and
- accept personal liability in the event of a breach of trust or other wilful default or in the event of loss being caused to the charity by acting beyond the powers given to them in the governing instrument.

Although the Companies Acts and Insolvency Acts impose specific duties on the directors of charitable companies limited by guarantee, these duties are consistent with the duties imposed on charity trustees generally.

Duties and responsibilities

Broadly, the main legal duties of a governor are:

- to carry out activities that are calculated to promote the objects for the benefit of the public;
- to observe the charity's constitution and act within its powers;
- to act in the best interests of their charity;
- to act with integrity and avoid any conflicts between personal interests and the interests of their charity;
- not to benefit personally from the charity except with express legal authority;
- to act personally and not delegate responsibility for decisions to anyone else;
- to ensure the charity is solvent and well run;
- to manage any risks to the charity, its assets and its reputation;
- to comply with charity law and the requirements of the Charity Commission as regulator;
- to have regard to other legal requirements;
- to use reasonable care and skill with regard to their personal skills and experience; and
- to take professional advice when needed.

Common problem areas

There are a number of common problem areas for governors which arise from the duties and responsibilities of charity trustees.

Delegation

Governors' powers may be delegated, but responsibility cannot. Decisions on day-to-day management matters should be delegated to the head, the bursar and other employees. The terms of delegation should be set out in writing and there should be a clear understanding as to which decisions should be reserved for the governors. However, the governors remain responsible for the acts and decisions of their delegates.

Conflicts of interest

It is inevitable that conflicts of interests or duties will occur from time to time. Governors have a duty to ensure that those conflicts are managed carefully to enable them to act solely in the best interests of the charity. Governors should therefore adopt a conflicts of interest policy, whose key elements should be to ensure that:

- conflicts and potential conflicts of interest are properly identified and disclosed; and
- conflicted governors do not participate in any decision by the governing body that relates to a matter on which they are conflicted.

Trustee benefits

Charity law prohibits governors from benefiting from their charity without express authority to do so. As charity trustees, they are expected to act voluntarily and without payment. Benefits do not include the reimbursement of properly incurred expenses, but expenses do not include compensation or loss of earnings.

Exceptions to this rule are where there is express authority for certain benefits set out in the charity's constitution, available as a statutory right or granted by the Charity Commission.

Benefits authorised by the constitution vary from charity to charity, but typically include:

- reasonable interest on money loaned to the charity;
- reasonable rent on property leased to the charity; and
- payments to companies in which the governor owns less than 1 per cent of the share capital.

The Charities Act 2006 introduced two important statutory powers that are available provided there is nothing in the constitution that specifically forbids them applying:

- to make a reasonable payment to a governor for the supply of any services over and above usual trustee duties. Conflicts must be managed appropriately and the governors who take the decision must agree that the service is required by the charity and that it is in the charity's best interests to make the payment. The governors must comply with certain other conditions, including a requirement for the agreement to be in writing. Only a minority of governors can benefit in this way; and
- to pay premiums for trustee indemnity insurance, provided that the insurance does not cover any fines imposed in criminal proceedings; liabilities arising out of criminal proceedings in which the governor

is convicted of an offence of fraud, dishonesty or wilful or reckless misconduct; or liabilities arising from conduct the governor ought to have known was not in the interests of the charity.

Benefits not authorised by the constitution or by statute may be authorised in advance by the Charity Commission, but the commission does not have power to authorise payments retrospectively. If a benefit is received by a governor without authority, then that is a breach of trust and the governor concerned will be liable to repay the charity in full, with an obligation on the other governors to consider enforcing that liability.

These restrictions apply in the same way to anyone connected to a governor which typically includes:
- children, parents, grandchildren, grandparents, sibling, spouse or civil partner;
- professional partner (or a professional partner of a connected relation);
- an institution controlled by any of the above; and
- a body corporate in which the governor or any other connected party alone or together has more than 20 per cent of the voting rights.

Investments
There are several significant aspects to the duty owed by charity trustees when making investments. These are:
- to act within the scope of their investment powers;
- to have regard to the suitability of investments and the need for diversification;
- to obtain and consider proper advice;
- to review the charity's investments from time to time; and
- to exercise due care and skill, having regard to any special knowledge or expertise that the governors have.

Governors usually have powers to delegate the management of investments to a qualified investment manager. Governors of unincorporated charities have a statutory power to delegate the management of investments, but should ensure that the constitution of their charity does not restrict or exclude that power. Governors of incorporated charities should check there is an appropriate express power.

Trading
Charity law and tax law do not allow charities to generate more than £50,000 turnover from trading activities beyond those permitted by the charitable objects. Schools can get round this restriction with a properly established trading company which then gives its profits to the charity. However, common traps that risk liabilities for governors include:
- lack of powers to set up and run a trading subsidiary;
- inadequate contractual agreements between the charity and the trading

company and the trading company and third parties;

- unmanaged conflicts of interest between the directors of the trading company and governors; and
- dealing with investments in, or loans to, the trading company other than on commercial arm's length terms.

Governors' liabilities

Governors may be made personally liable for their acts and omissions in two different ways:

- a governor who does not comply with the duties s/he owes to the charity is personally liable to compensate the charity out of her or his own assets for the losses the charity would not have suffered if the breach of duty had not occurred. This is usually referred to as a "breach of trust" and will apply to the governors of any charity irrespective of whether it is incorporated or unincorporated; and
- a governor may be personally liable for the liabilities owed by the charity to third parties eg to the charity's employees, contractual counterparties or creditors. The scope for a liability of this kind arising will vary depending on whether the charity is incorporated or unincorporated.

Liability for breach of trust

In discharging their duties as charity trustees, the governors of every school (whether incorporated or unincorporated) are under an obligation to exercise the degree of care and skill that can reasonably be expected of them in relevant circumstances. The level of care and skill required is assessed as having regard to:

- any special knowledge or expertise that the governor has (or holds her or him as having); and
- where the governor acts in the course of a business or profession, to any special knowledge or expertise that it would be reasonable to expect of a person acting in the course of that kind of business or profession.

While this obligation does not require a governor to meet a wholly objective standard of skill and experience, it does not impose a wholly subjective test (which would only require a governor to meet her or his own standards of skill and experience).

How can liability for breach of trust be managed and limited? There are three important points:

- governors should ensure that they understand the duties they owe and (where necessary) take advice;
- governors will generally be able to take out indemnity insurance against their own liabilities for breach of trust (provided their charity's constitution allows them to do so). There are limits on the scope of cover that can be obtained, particularly for breaches of trust that arise because

of conduct the governors knew (or ought to have known) was not in the interest of the charity. (As with most insurance cover, the devil is in the detail); and

- the Courts or the Charity Commission may decide that a governor who has acted honestly and reasonably should be excused any personal liability.

Liability for acting ultra vires
If the governors act outside the powers available to them as charity trustees (and in the case of companies, as directors) then they can be held personally liable for any resulting loss to the school.

Liability for health and safety issues
Liability for health and safety issues falls both on the school (however constituted) and on individual governors. Enforcement action will depend on the legal structure of the charity. If the charity is incorporated, it can be prosecuted in the corporate name. If unincorporated, the governors should be prosecuted in their own names as trustees.

An individual governor can be held criminally responsible for health and safety offences where:

- the body corporate itself is found guilty of a health and safety offence; and
- the offence was committed with the consent or connivance, or was attributable to any neglect on the part, of the governor.

The appointment of a single governor with named responsibility for health and safety does not alter the potential liability of all governors for health and safety issues.

The Health and Safety Executive's enforcement policy statement states: "Enforcing authorities should identify and prosecute or recommend prosecution of individuals if they consider that a prosecution is warranted. In particular, they should consider the management chain and the role played by individual directors and managers, and should take action against them where the inspection or investigation reveals that the offence was committed with their consent or connivance or to have been attributable to neglect on their part and where it would be appropriate to do so in accordance with this policy. Where appropriate, enforcing authorities should seek disqualification of directors under the Company Directors Disqualification Act 1986."

Questions that may be relevant include:

- did the governor have effective control over the matter?
- did s/he have (or ought s/he to have had) knowledge of the circumstances surrounding the event?
- did s/he fail to take obvious steps to prevent the event?
- has s/he had previous advice/warnings?

- was there previous advice to the charity? and
- is responsibility shared between more than one level of management?

Manslaughter and corporate manslaughter

A governor can also face individual liability for manslaughter if s/he commits the common law offence of manslaughter when s/he causes death through gross negligence. To be culpable, the jury must be satisfied that:

- the governor owed a duty of care to the deceased;
- there had been a breach of this duty of care; and
- the breach was so grossly negligent that the governor can be deemed to have had such disregard for the life of the deceased that the governor's conduct should be seen as criminal and deserving of punishment.

Prosecutions of directors or governors for common law manslaughter, however, are extremely rare and hard to secure.

The Corporate Manslaughter and Corporate Homicide Act 2007 came into force on 6 April 2008. This introduced a new offence of corporate manslaughter. This arises where an organisation's senior managers manage or organise its activities in a way that causes a person's death. The act relates to the culpability of an organisation as a whole and governors cannot be held individually liable under the act.

For a school to be guilty of the offence of corporate manslaughter, the test is if the way in which its activities are managed or organised amounts to a gross breach of a duty of care and causes a person's death.

The term "senior management" is defined to mean those people who play a significant role in the management of the whole or a substantial part of the organisation's activities and will, therefore, include governors. It is intended to include the direct chain of management as well as those in, for example, strategic or regulatory compliance roles.

It is anticipated that fines under the act could amount to 2.5-10 per cent of turnover and are payable by the charity rather than governors personally.

Liability to third parties

The liability of governors to third parties will depend primarily on whether their charity is incorporated or unincorporated.

Unincorporated charities

The governors of an unincorporated charity are potentially personally liable for all liabilities to third parties. This will include liabilities in contract (eg to parents, landlords, suppliers, the bank) and in tort (eg to those injured as a result of negligence). This is because an unincorporated charity has no legal personality of its own and can only interact with third parties via its governors.

This means that the governors themselves take on liabilities to third parties personally. In other words, they are potentially personally liable to meet the liabilities in question.

Generally speaking, the governors will not have to meet the liabilities out of their own assets because they can indemnify themselves for properly incurred liabilities out of their charity's assets. That indemnity will often be an express provision in the charity's constitution. Failing that, there is an implied indemnity under the Trustee Act 2000.

This means that there are two circumstances in which the governors of an unincorporated charity may have personal liability:
- where the charity's assets are not sufficient to meet the liabilities due to a third party; or
- where the liability in question has not been properly incurred by the governors in the first place, so that the governors cannot rely on the indemnity (the usual example is a liability incurred as a result of a breach of trust by the governors eg borrowing where there is no power to do so).

Trustees may seek to limit their potential liability in a number of ways:
- contractual liabilities may be limited by agreeing with the counterparty that their recourse for breach of contract is limited to the charity's assets from time to time; or
- liability for negligence may be limited by insurance, depending on the scope and extent of the available cover (again, the devil is in the detail).

As previously indicated, the trustees of an unincorporated charity can obtain a certificate of incorporation under Part VII of the Charities Act 1993, enabling them to sue and be sued and also to hold land in their corporate name. A certificate does not, however, confer limited liability on the trustees of an unincorporated charity.

As also previously indicated, the trustee of an unincorporated charity can itself be an incorporated body. A corporate trustee may be appointed by the Charity Commission or pursuant to powers in the charity's governing instrument. Where a corporate trustee is appointed, it will have all of the usual duties and liabilities of a charity trustee. Its directors (who might otherwise be the charity's trustees) will not be charity trustees, but they will owe fiduciary duties to the corporate trustee in managing the way in which it functions as a charity trustee.

If the corporate trustee is in breach of its duties to the charity, only the trustee itself will be directly liable as a result, but the trustee may have claims against its directors personally for the losses it suffers as a result. Bearing in mind the other disadvantages of using a corporate trustee, it is unlikely to assist governors materially with minimising their risk of personal liability.

Incorporated charities

Incorporated charities confer "limited liability" status on their members. This means that the liabilities a charity incurs are liabilities of the charity itself; any claim is limited to the assets of the charity itself and, in most circumstances, cannot be enforced against the charity's members personally. These are usually the governors.

A charity that is a limited company owes its limited liability status to the Companies Acts. A corporation's limited liability status derives from common law or the Act of Parliament by which it is constituted.

There are some circumstances in which the governors of an incorporated charity may be personally liable to third parties. The most significant potential liability is for "wrongful trading". Liability arises where the charity goes into insolvent liquidation and, before the start of the liquidation, the governors knew (or ought to have known) that there was no reasonable prospect that the charity would avoid insolvent liquidation.

If the charity's liquidator can show that this is the case and that the governors did not subsequently take every step to minimise the loss to the charity's creditors, s/he can apply to the Court for an order for the governors to contribute to the charity's assets to make up any shortfall in losses that have resulted after the date on which the governors knew or ought to have known that the charity would become insolvent.

In practice, and in the absence of any dishonesty (which is likely to give rise to a claim of "fraudulent trading"), the governors of a charity in financial difficulty will be most concerned about liability for wrongful trading. The key steps in managing this risk are:
- taking legal and financial advice at an early stage;
- ensuring that the financial information required to make judgements about the charity's finances are up-to-date and accurate; and
- assessing the situation regularly and ensuring that all deliberations and decisions are properly recorded.

Insurance

Notwithstanding the limited liability status of their charity, some governors should consider insuring against certain liabilities:
- specific liabilities owed by the charity to third parties (eg public liability insurance, professional indemnity insurance or insurance against business interruption); and
- the governors' own liabilities (indemnity insurance). There are limits on the scope of indemnity insurance paid for by the charity, which must not cover liability for fines, the cost of unsuccessfully defending criminal proceedings or against fraud of "reckless" breaches of trust or (more significantly) losses arising out of conduct that the governors knew

(or must be assumed to have known) was not in the charity's interests. Governors should note that this final caveat may limit their ability to claim against an indemnity policy for liability for wrongful trading.

Chapter **7**

Key legislation: the Companies Act 2006 and Charities Act 2006 (including public benefit critique), and the Charities and Trustee Investment (Scotland) Act 2005: by Ewa Holender, Sam Macdonald and Simon Mackintosh

Companies Act 2006 and Charities Act 2006, by Ewa Holender and Sam Macdonald

Most independent schools are constituted as charitable companies. This chapter provides an overview of the main areas of both company and charity law that governors of those schools should bear in mind. Both areas of law have seen recent development and this chapter takes into account the changes made by the Companies Act 2006 and the Charities Act 2006.

For schools constituted other than as companies, for example by Charity Commission Scheme or by Royal Charter, the principles of charity law set out below apply equally, though company law does not (at least not to the same extent).

It is also worth remembering that even a school constituted as a charitable company may hold certain assets on trust (eg permanent endowment land or bursary funds). In those cases, trust law will apply in addition to the relevant requirements of charity and company law. Governors will need to treat the assets as trust assets, rather than as straightforward company property, and have regard to the terms of the trusts on which they are held.

As with all legal overviews, there is a caveat. This chapter is intended to be a necessarily brief synopsis; if you require further detail, it is important to seek professional advice.

Background

Charitable companies have a two-tier governance structure:
- the directors are responsible for the management of the company; and
- the members are responsible for certain long-term decisions, such as changes to the governing documents or the removal of directors.

The governors are the directors of the school for the purposes of company law, and its charity trustees under charity law. They are responsible for the management of the school.

The governors will also usually be the school's members and will make certain long-term decisions in that capacity. There may, however, be additional or entirely different members; sometimes a third party may be a school's sole (corporate) member.

The rules governing the administration of a school will be contained in its governing documents (for a charitable company, its memorandum and articles of association). Governors should ensure that they are familiar with these documents as they will be the first port of call for many questions.

Composition of the governing body

The Charity Commission generally requires charities to have a minimum of three trustees and recommends that there should be no more than 10 or 12 for a governing body to function effectively. However, school governing bodies are often larger than this.

Provisions regarding the tenure, nomination and appointment of governors differ widely between schools. Reference must be made to the articles. Any appointment or retirement of a governor must be notified to Companies House on form AP01 or TM01 respectively. Any change of a governor's details should also be notified, using form CH01.

Governors' duties

Although most day-to-day management will be carried out by the head and paid staff, the governors are ultimately responsible for the overall management of the school.

As trustees of a charity, the governors will have overriding charity law duties. Governors must act in the best interests of the school and in furtherance of its charitable objects. They must pursue the objects by exercising their constitutional powers as set out in the school's governing document and as provided by law (for example, the Trustee Act 2000, if the school is unincorporated or holds property on trust).

These duties apply where a school is a charity, regardless of its legal form. Where the school is a charitable company, the governors will have further (though, in many respects, similar) duties as directors.

The general duties applicable to governors of schools constituted as charitable companies are considered below. Many of these duties will apply equally in the case of any school that is a charity, regardless of its constitution.

Achievement of its charitable objects

In making any decision, the governors must have regard to a number of factors, including the likely long-term consequences of the decision, the need to foster good relationships with others (beneficiaries, supporters and the Charity Commission) and the impact of the school's operations on the community and the environment.

To exercise independent judgement

Governors must not subject their discretion to the will of others, including any body that nominated them or their fellow governors.

Where the articles allow it, the governing body may delegate its powers to a sub-committee, individual governor or the head. For example, schools often create a finance and general purposes committee and an educational committee, and identify individual governors with specific responsibilities. It should be emphasised that, notwithstanding any such delegation, all the governors remain accountable for any decisions or actions taken. Any individual or committee to whom powers have been delegated must report any action or decision to the governing body on a regular basis.

The articles may provide that a minimum number of committee members must be governors, and it is good practice to set out the committee's role and responsibilities in detailed terms of reference.

The school's governing documents and all relevant legislation
The governors must ensure that the school does not breach any of the requirements or rules set out in its memorandum and articles, and that it remains true to the charitable purpose and objects set out there. Governors must act in accordance with the powers in the school's memorandum and articles and only use those powers to further the school's charitable objects.

Governors are also responsible for ensuring that the school complies with charity law, and with the requirements of the Charity Commission as a regulator; in particular, that the school prepares reports on what it has achieved and annual returns and accounts as required by law (see section on accounts and reports below).

Governors must comply with the requirements of other legislation and other regulators (if any) that govern the activities of the school.

Act with integrity
The governors must not place themselves in a position where the interests of the school conflict (or are likely to conflict) with other interests or duties. This duty covers a broad range of situations: for example, where a governor is paid for services provided to the school or is the parent of a pupil.

The governing body should put in place a conflicts of interest policy to provide governors with guidance on the appropriate procedure for declaring and managing conflicts. This should provide, inter alia, that any governor who has a conflict or potential conflict should declare that interest, withdraw from the meeting and not vote on the matter in question.

Governors must declare (in writing or orally) any direct or indirect interest in a proposed transaction with the school before the school enters into the transaction, and any interest in an existing transaction or arrangement as soon as reasonably possible.

A conflicted governor can only act if the articles specifically allow the conflict in question, or the conflict is authorised by the school's members (in practice, often its governors). From 1 October 2008, a school's articles may also give non-conflicted governors, in their capacity as directors, the power to authorise conflicts. Articles of schools incorporated before 1 October 2008 are unlikely to contain such provision, and schools in this position may wish to consider making an amendment to include this power for administrative ease.

Governors may be reimbursed for reasonable expenses. Unless the articles forbid it, they may also receive reasonable remuneration for services provided to the school (or goods supplied in connection with such services), but only if specific conditions set out in the Charities Act 1993 are met. These require a written agreement between the school and the governor, that the governors believe the remuneration is in the best interests of the school, that no more than half of the governors are remunerated at any time and that there is no prohibition on remuneration in the articles.

Any other conflict that would allow a governor to receive a material benefit from the school must be authorised by a specific provision in the articles, the Charity Commission or the Court. "Benefit" includes any property, goods or services that have a monetary value, as well as money. It will include certain indirect benefits: for example, where a trustee's spouse or other close relative is employed by the school.

Not to abuse their position as governors to benefit themselves
A governor must not accept benefits from third parties that are offered to her or him either because s/he is a governor or as a reward for doing (or not doing) something in her or his capacity as such. This duty will not be breached if accepting the benefit cannot reasonably be regarded as likely to give rise to a conflict of interests for the governor concerned.

To act prudently
Governors must ensure that the charity is and will remain solvent, and use charitable funds and assets reasonably, and only in furtherance of the charity's objects. This means they should avoid undertaking activities that might place the charity's endowment, funds, assets or reputation at undue risk, and should take special care when investing the funds of the charity, or borrowing funds for the charity to use.

The standard of care expected of governors
Company and charity legislation set out different standards of care for directors and charity trustees, but the requirements are broadly similar. This means that, while both standards will apply to the governors of schools constituted as charitable companies, in practice compliance with one test will usually also satisfy the other.

When carrying out their duties, the governors, as directors, are expected to act with: "The care, skill and diligence that would be exercised by a reasonably diligent person with:
- the general knowledge, skill and experience that may reasonably be

expected of a person carrying out the functions carried out by the [governor] in relation to the [school]; and

- the general knowledge, skill and experience that the [governor] has."

More will be expected of a governor who has specialist experience: for example, one who is a certified accountant.

As charity trustees, the governors must use reasonable care and skill in their work, using their personal skills and experience to ensure that the school is well-run and efficient. They must consider getting external professional advice on all matters where there may be material risk to the school, or where the governors may be in breach of their duties.

Although one of the advantages of incorporation is that governors enjoy limited personal liability, they can be held personally liable in circumstances where they have acted fraudulently or negligently. Personal liability may also be incurred in certain specific situations: for example, where the governors have committed a breach of trust or where the school has failed to pay tax or National Insurance contributions. Personal liability is a particular concern where a school may be insolvent; governors should proceed with extra caution in such circumstances and act only with appropriate advice.

Meetings and resolutions
Governors (as directors)
Subject to the articles, it is up to the governors to decide how often they should meet, although it is recommended that meetings are held regularly. Most governing bodies meet once per term, but some find it useful to meet more often. Written minutes of discussions and decisions taken at governing body meetings must be made, approved by the governors, signed by the chair and kept for at least ten years.

Notice of a proposed meeting must be given to all the governors. The articles of association will specify the minimum number of governors that must be present at a meeting (ie the quorum). Resolutions are passed by a majority of those present and voting. In the event that the governors are evenly divided on any proposal, the chair will have a casting vote (if the articles so provide). The articles may require certain decisions to be made by unanimous vote and certain decisions are reserved by law to the members of the school (who are often the governors acting in a different capacity).

If it is not practicable for all the directors to meet, then – if the articles allow it – a written resolution signed by all or a majority of the governors indicating their consent is sufficient and constitutes a valid decision.

Members
In most cases, the governors will be the same individuals as the members of the school. This means that, in addition to their roles as directors, they are also responsible for certain long-term decisions that are reserved to the

members, such as amendments to the articles, and will need to make those decisions in their capacity as members.

Private companies (which will include charitable schools) are no longer required to hold an annual general meeting (AGM), although they can choose to do so, and the articles may require it. Where the school has members other than the governors, an AGM is valuable in keeping everyone involved and informed. On the other hand, if the governors perform both roles, a school may wish to cease holding AGMs (and remove any requirement for AGMs in the articles).

Members may make decisions in general meetings or by resolution in writing. The articles will set out rules for the conduct of meetings, quorum provisions and the methods that can be used to give notice or communicate written resolutions. Notice of any general meeting must be given to all members, governors and the auditors. The length of notice is 14 days, unless a longer period is specified by the articles. Shorter notice can be given with the agreement of at least 90 per cent of the members (or any higher percentage specified in the articles, up to 95 per cent).

Written resolutions no longer have to be unanimous, and will be passed as an ordinary resolution when approved by the majority or as a special resolution when approved by 75 per cent of the members. A written resolution will automatically lapse if not passed within the timescale specified in the articles. In the absence of any provision in the articles, the standard timescale is 28 days after circulation.

Accounts and reports
Annual accounts: charitable companies
The governors are responsible for preparing annual accounts, to the same date in each year, and filing these at Companies House. The period allowed for filing is nine months from the end of the relevant accounting period (ten months for accounting periods beginning before 6 April 2008). It is an offence to deliver accounts late and fines are levied for late filing.

Annual report
The governors are also responsible for producing a directors' report, which is usually attached to the school's annual accounts. It must contain certain statutory information (including the public benefit provided by the school) and must be submitted to Companies House with the accounts.

Annual return
The governors must also file an annual return (Form AR01) with Companies House, within 28 days after the anniversary of incorporation or the anniversary of the date to which the last annual return was made up. Failure to file the annual return on time is an offence and fines can be imposed on directors for non-filing.

Charity Commission

For charitable schools (assuming gross income exceeds £25,000) the accounts, annual report and an annual return (in the form specified by the Charity Commission) must also be sent to the commission within 10 months of the end of the relevant financial year.

Independent scrutiny

The level of independent scrutiny of a charitable school's accounts will depend upon its income and assets:

Income	Independent scrutiny
Less than £10,000	None
£10,000–£100,000	Examination by an independent person who is reasonably believed by the trustees to have the requisite ability and practical experience
£100,000–£250,000	Independent examination as above, unless the school has assets greater than £3.26 million (£2.8 million in relation to any financial year ending before 1 April 2009), in which case an audit is required
£250,000–£500,000	Independent examination by a qualified examiner, unless the school has assets greater than £3.26 million
More than £500,000	Audit (see section on auditors below)

Submission of accounts to members

The governors must send copies of the annual accounts, the annual report and the auditor's report to the school's members and anyone entitled to receive notice of general meetings. There is no longer a need for the accounts to be presented at a general meeting, unless the articles require this.

Public access

The governors as charity trustees must make a copy of the school's most recent accounts and annual report available to anyone who makes a request in writing. A reasonable fee may be charged.

Auditors

Auditors must be appointed for each financial year unless the governors reasonably believe audited accounts are unlikely to be required. Under new provisions of the Companies Act 2006, the incumbent auditors are deemed reappointed each year unless, among other things, the articles require actual reappointment or the members give notice to prevent the reappointment. It is important to note, however, that where auditors were originally appointed by the directors, the automatic reappointment provisions will not apply; the appointment will need to be made by the members before automatic reappointment applies.

Any provision exempting an auditor from liability in connection with negligence, default, breach of duty or breach of trust is void, except insofar as it provides an indemnity for costs of successfully defending proceedings or complies with specific provisions for liability-limitation agreements.

Liability-limitation agreements may cap the liability of an auditor but require the prior approval of the members, must only relate to one financial year and will not be binding unless they are "fair and reasonable in the circumstances". Governors will need to consider whether agreeing to cap the auditors' liability will be in the best interests of the school.

Constitutional changes

Changes to a school's memorandum and articles of association must be made by way of a special resolution (ie 75 per cent or more) of the members. The school's governing documents may specify more stringent conditions for changing certain provisions: for example, a requirement of unanimity.

In addition, the consent of the Charity Commission will be required for certain "regulated alterations" (pursuant to section 64 of the Charities Act 1993). These comprise any alteration of the objects, provisions directing the application of property on dissolution or any alteration that would provide authorisation for any benefit to be obtained by the governors (as directors) or members of the school, or persons connected with them.

The procedure for changing the governing documents of schools constituted other than as companies will usually be set out in the governing documents.

Public benefit

The Charities Act 2006 removed the longstanding presumption in law that charities with aims to advance education are for the public benefit. According to the Charity Commission, this means that a charitable independent school must now be able to show that it provides a clear, identifiable benefit, related to its aims, to the public or a sufficient section of the public.

Charity Commission guidance

The commission has published extensive guidance on public benefit, which is available via its website (**www.charity-commission.gov.uk**).

Governors have a statutory duty to have regard to the relevant guidance, particularly the commission's general guidance on public benefit (Charities and Public Benefit) and its supplemental guidance on advancement of education and on fee-charging (The Advancement of Education for the Public Benefit, and Public Benefit and Fee-charging).

The following sections provide a summary of the principles set out in the guidance.

Benefits must be related to aims

The guidance indicates that public benefit will be assessed by reference to a school's activities. Only benefits that are related to the school's aims will be taken into account. For example, if the aims of a school are to promote education, the commission will not take into account any public benefit that arises from its conservation of architecturally important school buildings. Similarly, if a school's aim is to educate boys and the boys run a lunch club for old people in their community, the benefit to the boys, as part of their broader education will count, but any benefits to the old people will not count towards the school's public benefit as this benefit is not linked to running a school.

The Advancement of Education for the Public Benefit guidance includes an annex setting out what the commission considers does and does not fall within the aims of a typical school (and therefore what it will take into account in making any public benefit assessment).

The annex is not entirely helpful as it states that what an aim to run a school means is a matter for the governors. However, in practice, it seems that the commission will accept that ancillary and incidental educational activities will count, but that other associated activities for the benefit of the community will not.

This is one of a number of points of controversy in the commission's approach to public benefit (see critique later).

Governors should consider whether the aims of the school are adequately expressed in the school's objects clause and, if not, consider seeking amendments.

Restrictions on benefits

Benefits must be provided to the public or a section of the public. Restrictions on who has the opportunity to benefit are permitted, provided they are justifiable, proportionate and relevant to the aims of the school. For example, (according to the commission) an entrance exam is reasonable where those below a certain level of academic ability would not be able to reap the full benefits of education at the school, but an exam in Latin may not be reasonable because it could be used as a means of (unreasonable) exclusion.

Fees

Charities, including independent schools, are entitled to charge fees. However, the commission's guidance states that fee-charging charities must provide sufficient opportunities to benefit in a material way, that is related to the charity's aims, for people who cannot afford the fees, including people in poverty. The higher the fees charged, the more a charity must do to widen access. The opportunity to benefit must be significant and more than a token, and the benefits offered must be related to the charity's aims.

The guidance stresses that the commission will consider each charity on its own merits and circumstances, taking into account the totality of measures put in place to allow people who cannot afford the fees to benefit. The commission has accordingly refused to impose a fixed percentage or ratios in relation to free or subsidised access.

The commission's guidance highlighted that, while general benefits to the public at large might be desirable and relevant in a broad sense, they are not relevant to the issue of providing opportunities to those who cannot afford the fees because they are not a material way of benefiting from the charity.

Private benefit

Private benefits are any benefits provided by a charity other than to a beneficiary: for example, salaries to employees. Private benefits are permitted but only provided they are incidental to a charity furthering its aims. For example, reduced fees for children of a school's teaching staff as a means of attracting good teachers could be incidental.

Public benefit reporting

Schools must include information about how they are carrying out their objects for the public benefit in annual reports for financial years starting on or after 1 April 2008.

Independent schools whose gross income exceeds £500,000 per annum must include a review of the significant activities undertaken by the school during the relevant financial year to further its charitable purposes for the public benefit or to generate resources to be used to further its purposes. Schools below this threshold must include a brief summary, setting out the main activities undertaken by the charity to further its charitable purposes for the public benefit. In addition, the annual reports of all charitable independent schools must contain a statement by the governors as to whether they have complied with the duty in section 4 of the Charities Act 2006 to have regard to the public benefit guidance published by the commission.

The commission has stated that it is for charity trustees to decide how much information and detail is appropriate given their charity's circumstances, but that a brief explanation with no detail will not suffice. For most governors, who should already be reporting on their activities, the new requirements should not significantly affect the existing structure of the annual report. Nevertheless, it would be sensible for governors to explain how their activities do deliver benefit to the public.

The commission has produced example annual reports, which include one prepared for a fictional fee-charging school, the Alltown School Foundation Charity. Governors may find this useful when preparing their own reports.

Critique of the public benefit requirements, by Sam Macdonald

The Charity Commission's first public benefit reports have received wide coverage in the press. The initial shocked reaction has subsided, but the consequences of the findings could be serious.

Three charities were judged to be failing to meet the test, and these included one care home charity and two independent schools. (A fourth, another care home, was deemed not to be operating within its objects, and so failed to get out of the public benefit starting blocks.)

All were fee-charging charities, and it is the impact of fee-charging on accessibility that attracted most of the commission's attention.

The commission's starting position is that if a charity charges high fees for its core services, there will be a significant proportion of the public that is excluded from the opportunity to benefit by dint of the fact that they cannot afford those fees. In its guidance on public benefit, the commission expressed the view that the best way to address this is to provide subsidised access to the charged-for services. It acknowledged that there would be other ways of providing broader public benefit, but it was fairly clear from the guidance that the commission viewed these as second best.

That approach has been applied in the live cases. The commission has placed great weight on the total value of bursaries that a school awards, as well as whether the school offers any fully-funded places. The three schools that passed the test awarded bursaries of between 5 per cent and 14 per cent of total fee income. Of the two that failed, one awarded bursaries worth less than 1 per cent of fee income and the other offered no bursary support at all. The three schools that passed also offered some (though not necessarily very many) fully-funded places. Neither of the two failed schools did this.

Looking at fee assistance in isolation, then, the commission's findings are unsurprising. But public benefit as a legal concept is more complex and flexible than that.

Both of the schools that failed operate partnerships with local schools and other projects designed to provide educational opportunities to children other than their pupils. Indeed, the commission accepted that these programmes did provide broader public benefit in a way that was compatible with the schools' objects. But it ruled that they did not go far enough.

In a recent letter to schools, the commission has stressed that there is no fixed threshold in terms of the value of bursaries or number of fully-funded places. That may be so, but it does appear that the commission regards means-tested fee assistance as an essential component for any fee-charging charity. Whatever the policy reasons for such an approach, it is not a principle that appears in the law.

The commission refutes the suggestion that introducing or enhancing a bursary programme will necessarily lead to higher fees. However, in the case of one of the schools that failed, the annual fees were kept deliberately low so that they were affordable to as many people as possible. It is hard to see how the introduction of a bursary programme would not lead to an increase in fees at such a school, which of course would disrupt the affordability principle. It must be hoped, therefore, that the commission can be persuaded to recognise that the ways in which the broader public can benefit are many and varied, and that there is value in letting schools (and other charities) decide which work best for them.

An overview of the Charities and Trustee Investment (Scotland) Act 2005 and public benefit in Scotland, by Simon Mackintosh

The Charities and Trustee Investment (Scotland) Act 2005 was revolutionary in scope. Scotland has never had a Charity Commission, nor anything like it: Inland Revenue (Claims Branch) was responsible for granting charitable status. The Lord Advocate, latterly with some powers gained in 1990 and operating through the Scottish Charities Office, was responsible for dealing with misconduct. Now, we have the Office of the Scottish Charity Regulator (OSCR), responsible for dealing with misconduct and maintaining the Scottish Charity Register. All Scottish charities need to be on this. To be on the register, they have to pass a statutory "charity test", which is in two main parts: relating to their charitable purposes and to the provision of public benefit.

New measures

When the 2005 act came into force, all existing known Scottish charities were moved onto the register at its inception. The Rolling Review carried out by OSCR can be seen as a legal audit of a charity's purposes, activities and delivery of public benefit against this charity test.

Section 7 of the act provides that a body meets the charity test if its purposes consist only of one or more of the charitable purposes in the act; and it provides public benefit in Scotland or elsewhere (or, in the case of an applicant, intends to do so).

Section 8 of the act confirms the new rule that no particular purpose is to be presumed for the public benefit. It stipulates that, in determining whether public benefit is provided, regard must be given to:
- private benefit;
- public disbenefit compared with public benefit; and
- whether there is any unduly restrictive condition on obtaining that benefit (including any charge or fee).

This is an "on balance" test, based on the overall activities of the charity.

Roll on

Shortly after assuming its powers, OSCR started its Rolling Review programme and identified independent schools as a priority area, based on a risk of failing the public benefit test.

An initial pilot study into a range of charities included one independent school, the High School of Dundee, which was found to provide public benefit. A relevant factor was the level of bursary support, which was clearly well established and integrated into the school's culture.

OSCR then embarked on Phase IA of its Rolling Review, which covered a further 30 charities, of which 11 were independent schools, representing a wide range of the sector. The Phase IA report was issued in October 2008 and is worth studying, not only in reference to the schools considered.

OSCR states: "A clear conclusion from the process has been that means-tested access arrangements have the most significant impact on opening up access that is restricted due to fees that are being charged."

OSCR also concluded that, in most cases, other kinds of benefits provided by schools were "neither significant enough nor closely enough related to the charity's purposes to have critical impact in our assessment of public benefit". By this, it means activities including contributions to teacher training, curriculum development, access to facilities and the like. It may well be that this type of public benefit needs to be better understood by the sector.

OSCR's report contains a number of case summaries, including reports on some of the schools reviewed. It is clear that OSCR's approach varies according to the level of fees and, therefore, the need to mitigate them. In one case (the Regius School), OSCR found that the school sought to make sure that access was open to a wide range of beneficiaries by keeping all fees as low as possible, by using donated and grant income and minimising costs. This was thought to be an appropriate strategy to enable those on a range of incomes to benefit. In another case (Glasgow Steiner School), the fees were targeted at the ability to pay, not only of those seeking assistance but of all potential beneficiaries. Again, this was thought to be an appropriate mechanism to mitigate barriers to entry.

In the case of George Heriot's School, 12 per cent of the school roll was supported on a means-tested basis; that support amounts to 9 per cent of the school's income. Again, OSCR found that although the fees charged were substantial, there were satisfactory arrangements to facilitate access.

On the other hand
On the other side of the dividing line, Merchiston Castle School has high fees with a substantial level of fee support, but not clearly means-related. Although the total value of fee support was just under 9 per cent of the total annual income, only 1.5 per cent was on a means-tested basis. Accordingly, the school was found not to provide public benefit.

The following should be noted:
- the absolute level of fees is significant in OSCR's determination of the type of mitigation arrangements it is looking for;
- the level of fees, compared with the cost of education in the state sector, is taken into account; and
- support from external sources can be taken into account, but only if it too is means-tested.

Three ways
OSCR issued innovative three-stage directions to the charities that were required to change. Within three months, they were required to indicate that they would comply with the directions; within twelve months, to produce a plan that demonstrated how they would provide public benefit; and, within three years of the making of the directions, they have to implement those plans.

OSCR recommends to the Scottish Government that it should have the power to vary directions to react to new evidence and changing circumstances and this is no doubt partly as a result of this exercise, which indicates the difficulty of making and policing directions where a change of behaviour (as opposed to a straightforward change of constitution) is required.

Chapter **8**

General information and guidance: How to make a governing body effective; Reviewing the governing body's accountability; Effective recruitment of new governors; Good governance in finding new governors; How to develop the overall talents of the governing body; Effective sub-committees and structures; Benchmarking; Mergers; Safeguarding vulnerable groups (vetting and barring scheme); School protection guidance; Handling a crisis: by various authors

How to make a governing body effective, by Andrew Maiden

A governing body plays an important part in the life of a school: an effective governing body usually means an effective school. It should, however, hold regular reviews of governance procedures to keep standards high.

Many governing bodies work in isolation. It is important for schools to take the time to review the effectiveness of their governing body. After all, just because things have been done in a particular way at the school for years doesn't necessarily mean that it represents good practice.

The governing body that thinks it knows it all is complacent and will ultimately fail the school. Headteachers and bursars who are happy with an unquestioning body should be concerned that the school management risks being less effective than it could be. Governors who ask questions will help keep heads and bursars on their toes and prevent them from becoming complacent too.

Regular reviews

As a matter of course, it is important to regularly appraise a governing body. Some of the net benefits of a performance review are that governors can:

- develop as a team with shared goals, albeit with different skills and contributions;
- voice concerns about how they operate and resolve them;
- reflect on their joint strengths and weaknesses (and seek how to overcome the weaknesses); and
- prioritise future activities and renew their commitment to the school.

The gentle touch

Reviews can be most effective when they are regularly timetabled. Thrusting a review onto a governing body without warning can create alarm and anger. It is best to introduce the idea gently by beginning with informal reviews of each meeting. The chair should ask questions such as:

- did the agenda cover all matters?
- was each agenda item dealt with properly?
- did governors concentrate on policy decisions and avoid being drawn into management issues?
- how effective was the governing body in covering the agenda as a team? and
- were governors provided with the appropriate information prior to the meeting to help them make informed decisions?

When setting up a review, there are several key considerations:

- the review is evolutionary and should not be measured by a static checklist;
- the review process itself should also be evolutionary, reflecting the school's character and future plans;
- the headteacher and bursar both ought to be involved in the review as the effectiveness or otherwise of the governing body impacts on both of them; and
- initial reviews should be of the governing body as a whole. Future reviews could be of individual governors, considering any areas of help they may require.

Looking forwards

Some of the objectives a typical governing body might agree include:

- improvement of background information to items on the agenda;
- introduction of new or temporary governors with a specialist background to support specific projects;
- simplification of management and financial data presented at the meeting;
- agreement of tools to measure the effectiveness of school management;
- consideration of the governance structure and, if necessary, revision of the governing instruments;
- clarification of the authorities delegated to sub-committees;
- introduction of a day away from school premises to develop long-term strategies; and
- reduction of standard running times for meetings.

Once the idea of a review has been accepted and absorbed into the running of the school, governors should respond positively as it clarifies their own and collective roles and, at the same time, should make them feel valued.

Reviewing the governing body's accountability, by Nick Sladden

Governing bodies should review their accountability arrangements to ensure they observe best practice. It is the responsibility of every school governing body to ensure that it is composed of an appropriate number of individuals with the effective breadth and depth of expertise. Having effective governance arrangements – due processes and procedures – has become increasingly important across the public, private and voluntary sectors, including independent schools.

Against this trend of striving to achieve the highest standards of governance, there is evidence from the past few years to suggest that governing bodies are becoming rationalised, with lower governor numbers. This has concentrated key decisions among a smaller number of individuals. Inevitably, this means more demands are now being placed on 21st century independent school governors.

The new era for governance

With the introduction of the Charities Act 2006, there is, of course, now even further need for independent schools to show that they are working for the public benefit. Thus schools are becoming more accountable for their impact on society at large. As a result, there is an increasing expectation on schools to demonstrate to society how well they are governed.

The growth of the internet and information in the public domain also increases the levels of accountability and transparency required for schools. Helpfully, the internet in turn has itself been a valuable source of information for governors to find practical help, tools and best practice guidance on improving governance arrangements within their own schools.

A model of good practice

One example is the National Governance Hub for England, which has many useful tools and templates (**www.governancehub.org.uk**). The Governance Hub is funded by a ten-year government initiative and its biggest impact has been the publication in June 2005 of Good Governance: A Code for the Voluntary and Community Sector (the Code). The Code was developed for use in the voluntary and community sectors and has become increasingly prevalent, particularly among charities. It can therefore be applied to independent schools.

Although adoption of the Code by governing bodies is voluntary, it is intended to reflect best practice. The Code itself is principles-based. Organisations that adhere to these principles should state as much in their annual reports. The governors' report would be a suitable place for schools to make such a disclosure.

Arguably, any adoption of the Code by schools will help to show that good governance arrangements are in place and should assist in demonstrating accountability to society at large, which should be advantageous in the new era of public benefit testing.

Well defined

At the heart of the Code, a definition of governance is offered as: "The systems and processes concerned with ensuring the overall direction, effectiveness, supervision and accountability of an organisation." Schools need to develop systems and processes to address the seven main principles underlying the Code, which are as follows:

1. governing body leadership;
2. the governing body in control;
3. the high performance governing body;
4. governing body review and renewal;
5. governing body delegation;
6. governing body and trustee integrity; and
7. governing body openness.

As well as following the principles of the Code, a governing body needs to ensure that it possesses the right mix of skills, experience and qualities to make it effective. The starting point in building an effective governing body is to review the attributes of existing governors.

Effective recruitment of new governors, by Nick Sladden

Recruiting new governors is a proven method of correcting any known weaknesses in the expertise of the governing body as a whole and has the additional benefit of enhancing what is already there. Hiring new governors can be the result of a "skills audit" that identifies the skills and experience required to bring the governing body to its full potential. On occasion, schools may need to consider factors in addition to the recruitment needs of the governing body alone. Many schools have subsidiary companies undertaking trading activities to ensure compliance with charity law and taxation rules. In these situations, a good governance approach is to appoint at least one person to be a director of the trading subsidiary, who is not a governor of the school, to help to ensure that each entity is provided with an individual who can be truly independent in their decision-making. The Charity Commission produces excellent guidance on the topic in its publication, CC30 Finding New Trustees, which is available to download from its website.

Having a clear understanding of the skills and experience needed in a governor is the first stage of recruitment and it is best practice to turn these requirements into a short job description. Some schools prefer the term "role description" rather than "job description" to more accurately reflect the level of remuneration involved.

Outline the roles

Role descriptions are helpful because they help to forewarn prospective governors of the school's expectations and the ongoing commitment. Two essential words that have so far been missing from this essay are "time" and "energy". Despite predictions made in the 1980s, when it was thought that people would have more leisure time, the reverse seems to be the case. Therefore, schools cannot afford to recruit governors who do not appreciate the commitment involved or treat their position as purely honorary. However, it is worth the effort to accommodate and support the needs of busy people as they are often the ones who provide the best skills or experience.

Being flexible by arranging governing body meetings at convenient times and days of the week, meeting travel costs (if permitted) and providing allowances for childcare, all may help in persuading the right people that they will be able to contribute to the required degree. Energy and enthusiasm in potential candidates is not something that can be achieved with the help of the school. In many ways, it is the individual's level of self-motivation and enthusiasm that may help to define successful candidates.

Different approaches

At the outset, it is important that the governing body appreciates that, although certain tasks in the recruitment process can be delegated to staff, the governors must retain overall control of recruitment. The type of process used will depend on the size and structure of the school. Generally, smaller prep schools are going to require a relatively straightforward recruitment process, with individual governors taking on the responsibility. Larger senior schools may aim to be more formal and establish a nominations committee.

Currently, there are more than a million people in the UK who are either governors of independent schools or trustees of charities. Consequently, finding good-calibre candidates with sufficient time available to volunteer is not going to be easy. Traditionally, appointments to governing bodies have been via word of mouth; research shows that this is still one of the most favoured approaches. However, the Charity Commission's preferred method is through advertising as this provides a greater range of candidates with a wider array of skills and experience.

The concern is that too many charities are placing too much reliance on recruitment methods that are narrower and more passive than they could and should be. Most schools are unlikely to require the national press to advertise for new governors, which is fortunate given that cost can be prohibitive. Instead, school newsletters, alumni, local noticeboards, the school's website, parents' groups and the local press are likely to be good sources for advertising vacancies. Frequently, a skills audit will have identified a need for specialist skills and, in these situations, it may be appropriate to advertise for new governors in specialist press publications or trade journals as a way of improving the probability of finding the right candidate with the right skills. Given charity law restrictions, it is generally sensible to steer clear of using existing employees as a potential pool of governors.

Occasionally, the needs of a school cannot be met through advertising alone. The Association of Governing Bodies of Independent Schools holds a list of potential governors which mainly consists of former heads and governors. Alternatively, registers of potential trustees (governors) are maintained by organisations such as the Trustee Brokerage Network (operated by the National Council for Voluntary Organisations) and the Ethnic Minority Foundation. Online matching services are also available through **www.do-it.org.uk**.

Making the numbers
These methods should provide enough candidates to arrive at a suitable shortlist for interviews. There are three golden rules for the interview process: keep the panel small (to be effective), ask similar questions to each candidate (to ensure fairness) and retain notes (for accountability). If the panel is able to appoint, then it should be remembered that unsuccessful candidates should be notified in good time and thanked for their interest. Do not forget that for some candidates this may be their only opportunity to gain an impression about the school and it is best to make the experience a positive one.

But what if the process fails? The answer could be that there are alternatives to recruiting a governor, including arranging formal training for existing governors to cover any identified weaknesses, buying-in any missing expertise or co-opting individuals with specific skills on to sub-committees. Otherwise the search will need to continue.

Good governance in finding new governors, by Nick Sladden
Finding suitable new governors who can bring additional skills and experience is not easy, but with a robust process it can also bring an improved breadth and depth of skills to the governing body. It is therefore possible to become a little complacent once that new person has been found and forget that inevitably there are administrative tasks that need to be completed to achieve sound governance.

According to the Charity Commission, charitable independent schools should "before appointing a trustee...obtain a declaration from the prospective trustee that they are not disqualified [from acting as trustee]".

The guidance goes on to recommend that charities should also check official registers to confirm whether the proposed governor could be legally disqualified from acting as a trustee. People who are legally ineligible to act as trustees include bankrupts, disqualified directors and persons who have previously been removed as a charity trustee. Details of how to find the lists of bankrupts and disqualified directors can be found at **www.insolvency. gov.uk** and **www.companieshouse.gov.uk**.

Readers wishing to determine persons who have been previously removed as a charity trustee would need to review the registers (held separately from the Register of Charities) at each of the Charity Commission's offices.

These registers identify trustees removed from office (by the Charity Commission since 1961 or by the Courts since 1993) under the Charities Act 1993. Staff at the Charity Commission (contact details are available from **www.charity-commission.gov.uk**) advise on whether an individual is on the list if a name is supplied for them to check.

Academic staff will be familiar with the checks (including the Enhanced CRB checks) administered by the Criminal Records Bureau. Some may also be aware of the Independent Safeguarding Authority (ISA) that oversees the Vetting and Barring Scheme (launched in October 2009). Under the compulsory Scheme, the ISA administers two new barring lists – the Children's Barred List and the Adults' Barred List (replacing the lists that had been created under the Protection of Children Act (POCA) and List 99 of the Education Act). An ISA check will determine whether an individual is ISA-registered. Being ISA-registered means that the ISA has no known reason why the applicant should not work with children. Checks against these lists can also be made as part of an Enhanced CRB check.

Although unpopular, the ISA has a legal basis for the checking procedure, so (unless withdrawn or modified by a future administration) it is important to abide by the regulations. For the latest status of this controversial piece of legislation, visit **www.isa-gov.org.uk**.

As a minimum, the governing body should ask new governors to sign a declaration to confirm that they are not disqualified from acting as a charity trustee.

Ensuring governors know what is expected

To have an effective governing body that understands its legal responsibilities and the distinction between governance and management, it is helpful if governors are issued with a statement that defines their duties and responsibilities.

This statement should ensure that both governors and management understand their remits and the implications of their actions on their legal position. More specifically, it is helpful to ask all governors to sign and return a statement or letter that sets out their duties and responsibilities, and the expectations of the school on governors. The letter should, as a minimum, include obligations to:

- uphold the values and objectives of the school;
- give adequate time and energy to the duties of being a governor; and
- act with integrity, and avoid or declare personal conflicts of interest.

By its nature, a governor contract will need tailoring to individual schools and governors. Specimens of contracts are widely available from the internet (including at **www.ncvo-vol.org.uk**) and should be amended to suit each individual school's needs before issuing to governors.

Some readers may also be familiar with codes of conduct, which are simply a variation on governor contracts but which achieve the same aim. This common aim is to provide governors with clear guidelines for standards of behaviour, responsibilities, and best practice in fulfilling their obligations to the school. A code of conduct is a model of best practice and would cover areas such as selflessness, integrity, objectivity, accountability, openness, honesty and leadership.

How to develop the overall talents of the governing body, by Nick Sladden

Using a skills audit to identify the existing attributes of governors is a good starting point to ensure the balance of talents a school's governing body needs, as well as helping to identify any deficiencies. The skills audit process involves the use of a questionnaire, with governors scoring their individual expertise against a predetermined list of skills. Usually, the scoring is on a scale of 1 to 5, where 1 is a "limited degree of expertise" and 5 is "expert".

What does it mean?

Once all governors have completed their questionnaires, the results should be analysed. The simplest way of doing this is with a spreadsheet; enter the skills from the specimen questionnaire in the first column and map the scores for each governor in subsequent columns. The spreadsheet can then be used to determine the high scores for each area of expertise, allowing the school to identify where skills shortages may exist. It is essential that areas of expertise can be demonstrated by the governing body, even if a particular expertise rests with just one person.

Comparing apples to pears

Understanding the areas of expertise that have not recorded high scores makes it possible to identify whether there are areas of weakness. However, another factor to consider is the scoring approaches undertaken by different people. One governor may score a 4, whereas a second governor with a similar level of expertise may only score a 3. Marginal differences such as this are unlikely to cause problems, but it becomes a bigger issue as the breadth of scoring increases.

It is vital that the individual responsible for the process reviews the responses to ensure that they are reasonable and don't carry rogue results. For instance, it would be anticipated that most governors would score highly in a few areas, but record no score in others. In one skills audit, a governor scored every area of expertise on the questionnaire as 3. In another example, a governor recorded no scores in any individual area, but instead added his own category of "common-sense" and scored this as 5. Neither approach was helpful to the process!

It is critical to the success of the audit that all responses are balanced. If rogue responses are identified, it is worth discussing those scores with governors and revising their results. For governors intent on scoring every area highly, it is worth emphasising that the ideal governor would have every desirable skill and quality, yet in all likelihood we each have only a few.

When responses are reviewed, common-sense must prevail. It is impractical to provide too much detail in the questionnaire. For instance, "property" expertise could include an estate agent, quantity surveyor, architect, property manager, builder etc. Therefore, it will always be necessary to consider individual circumstances.

Looking to the future
Considering the possibility of governor retirements in the near future is imperative. Where they are pending, it is wise to re-compute the results of the audit and exclude the results of those governors. This will make it easier to identify whether short-term retirements from the governing body are likely to remove areas of expertise.

Effective sub-committees and structures, by Nick Sladden
An independent school is likely to have a number of formally constituted sub-committees that report directly to the main governing body. These sub-committees necessarily include selected governors but sometimes, where appropriate, have additional staff, parent or expert representation. However, the committee structure that is in place may not always be appropriate to the needs of the school and its governing body.

Sub-committee structures tend to evolve over time due to a perceived need and new sub-committees are added (or removed), usually over a number of years. As a result, the overall governance structure for a school can become inefficient as well as inappropriate to its strategic needs. This has become particularly apparent as governance best practice in the voluntary sector has developed significantly over the last ten years. Undertaking a review of organisational and trustee structures is also something that the Charity

Commission (see CC10 The Hallmarks of an Effective Charity) has been recommending for some time.

Stepping back

It is therefore good governance practice to undertake periodic reviews to take account of:

- the frequency of meetings of the governing body;
- the number of sub-committees and frequency of sub-committee meetings;
- any companies in which the school has an interest. For example, trading subsidiaries and its own board of directors; and
- the appropriate representation of staff, for instance, the head or bursar.

For effective management, the Charity Commission recommends that a minimum of two full governors' meetings are held in any 12-month period, where the business of a charity has to be transacted at meetings (see CC48 Charities and Meetings).

This should be achievable for all schools as many now operate a model where the governing body meets at least termly, with sub-committees of governors and senior management reporting back to the governing body at each meeting. The sub-committees lead the majority of the detailed work and report summaries of their findings to the governing body. To ensure that there is a clear differentiation between the roles of sub-committees and the governing body, each should have a clearly defined terms of reference.

Governors should ensure that they continue to be closely involved with strategic development and contribute regularly to high-level decisions within the school. Although sub-committees allow detailed work to be undertaken, there is a downside in that governors can inadvertently become too involved in management issues. However, governors by definition need to be involved with the school on a frequent yet timely basis.

The optimum length of time varies between meetings due primarily to the different sizes of schools, but anecdotal information suggests that a termly meeting over a morning or an afternoon maximises attendance. Where effective sub-committees are operating, governors are often involved on a six-weekly basis if sub-committee meetings are held in between governing body meetings.

One reason for advocating a simple and minimalist sub-committee structure is to avoid having a plethora of sub-committees that in practice result in the generation of reports from one sub-committee to another. This can be extremely inefficient and uses vital management time. In considering any new committee structure with a blank sheet of paper, it is also useful to insist that there is no more than one layer of sub-committee.

Making changes

At the time that any changes or a new structure is being determined, it is essential to make a commitment to review the operation of any new structure after it has been implemented for a period of six months to a year. This review gives the opportunity to determine whether the new structure is working in practice.

From time to time, the constitution of each sub-committee should also be reviewed and it is not always necessary to have a sub-committee made up entirely of experts. Frequently, it can be the layperson that asks the obvious or common-sense question on a sub-committee that sometimes gets missed by the experts. To achieve this, it is helpful to have a governing body that comprises a wide-range of skills and experience.

Some schools also maintain a register of individuals who may be past governors or simply have a close connection to the organisation. Such registers ("special interest registers") can be useful when particular expertise is required and the individuals with the requisite skills and experience can be called on by the governing body on an ad hoc basis. Typically these individuals may not wish to take on the commitment or responsibility of being a governor but are often prepared to offer help and advice from time to time. These individuals can then be co-opted onto sub-committees when there is a requirement for specific experience and expertise.

Benchmarking, by Andrew Maiden

Benchmarking is the process of identifying best practice in your school and comparing it with other, similar schools. Its objective is the evaluation of the school's current position to identify areas of improvement in performance.

Benchmarking involves four steps:
- understanding existing business processes of your school;
- analysis of business processes of other schools;
- comparison of business performance with that of other schools; and
- implementation of steps to improve your school's performance.

Benchmarking is not a one-off exercise. To be effective, it must become an ongoing, integral part of improvement. Types of benchmarking include: strategic, performance, process and functional. There are also internal and external benchmarking exercises.

Strategic benchmarking examines the long-term strategies and general approaches that have enabled the school to succeed. It involves aspects such as core competencies and improving capabilities for dealing with changes in the external environment. Changes from this type of benchmarking can be difficult to implement and may take a long time to materialise.

Performance benchmarking considers the school's position in relation to performance characteristics with other schools. This type of analysis is usually undertaken through third parties to protect confidentiality and for legal reasons.

Process benchmarking focuses on improving specific processes and operations. Benchmarking partners are sought from best practice organisations that perform similar work. Process benchmarking invariably involves process maps for comparison and analysis. This type of benchmarking usually results in short-term benefits.

Functional benchmarking is where partners are drawn from different business sectors to find ways of improving similar functions. This sort of benchmarking can lead to innovation and vast improvements.

Internal benchmarking involves analysing different parts of the school. The main advantage is that access to sensitive data and information is easier and is less time-consuming. However, innovation may not emerge from the results.

External benchmarking involves analysing other schools that are known to be excellent. This type of benchmarking can take up significant time and resources to ensure the comparability of data and information.

Benchmarking, by Noble Hanlon

Over the years, many independent schools have become aware of and are interested in comparisons with other, similar school operations to measure and gauge their operational activities. In many instances, this produces a useful comparison, but too often the conclusions are not always valid since the analysis for comparison is not necessarily drawn up on a consistent basis and, in the past, there has been much difficulty in obtaining relevant information. A survey by haysmacintyre (conducted for the last twenty-five years) enables schools to participate with other schools, based on seven groups.

Those groupings are separated between senior schools, preparatory schools and a combination of the two, whether they are day or boarding schools. Accordingly, there are groups for senior day, senior day with boarding, a combined senior and junior day group in addition to those that combine boarding and day. Also, there are preparatory schools which include either a day school group or a day school group with boarders. The purpose is to achieve more informed comparisons for the participating school with those within their constituent group.

The objective of the survey is to highlight the divergences of schools' costs from the average of a similar or comparable school. It should indicate particular costs where divergences from the average should either be justified in terms of the overall policy or the educational objective of the school. It is also important to ascertain whether cost savings could and should be made or whether the extent of additional expenditure is caused by policies or educational objectives that differ significantly from the average within the particular group.

In some instances, where a school appears to have costs in excess of the average, this should not be seen as a criticism of the school's efficiency. As an example: salary costs can be greatly affected by the policy on the size of forms and setting arrangements, the variety of sixth-form courses on offer or activities treated as extracurricular in the usual syllabus which, for some schools, are covered by the termly fee and hence are not charged as additional subjects. In addition, variations in policy will have an effect on the salary costs per pupil and, in some instances, the excess or otherwise around the average may in some cases be regarded as a course for congratulation rather than criticism, if there is a satisfactory explanation. To enable more meaningful comparisons, it is important to bear in mind that some costs may be more comparable between some schools than others.

Comparing like-for-like

In recent years, benchmarking has become increasingly popular between schools. However, the ruling by the Office of Fair Trading (OFT), which precludes schools from exchanging sensitive information on their financial performance, means that many schools have opted to take part in some of the recognised benchmarking surveys. If the survey data is collected and analysed by an independent third party, then there is no infringement of the OFT regulation. It is for this reason that governors should encourage participation by their schools in surveys to provide useful yardsticks for the analysis of financial and other performance.

The haysmacintyre survey includes an analysis of teaching, welfare, premise and administration costs, aggregating to the total operating costs with a number of individual cost-centre disclosures within those sub-totals. In addition, it includes information on pupil-teacher ratios, average teaching costs per member of staff and fee increases for the current and future year. There is also information on net outturns from operations and other statistical information, which is presented for each school in comparison with the descriptive group that it has chosen. The published survey produces more of a summary of the detail, whereas the individual results for the participating schools are in considerably more detail. This helps schools to consider their cost details and other operating statistics before decisions have to be made prior to budgeting and fee-setting cycles.

A tabulation of some of the latest results is detailed overleaf.

Survey results for independent schools:

Average costs	Senior schools					Preparatory schools	
	Boarding	Day/boarding	Day	Combined senior/junior day	Combined senior/junior day/boarding	Day/boarding	Day
	£	£	£	£	£	£	£
Teaching	9,391	8,542	6,659	5,538	6,237	6,500	5,410
Welfare	4,152	2,843	526	733	1,451	1,771	536
Premises	4,602	3,362	1,482	1,128	1,865	1,853	1,038
Administration	2,279	1,882	1,349	971	1,197	1,191	966
Total operating costs	£20,424	£16,629	£10,016	£8,370	£10,750	£11,315	£7,950
Pupil-teacher ratio	6.45	7.10	9.52	9.90	8.91	7.12	9.01

Source: haysmacintyre Management Survey for Independent Schools

Mergers: how governors can help, by Anthony Millard and Ben Brice

During hard times, it is not surprising to find independent schools facing significant reductions in pupil numbers as parents are no longer able to afford fees. Some schools are likely to face closure or seek a merger as the only viable way to stay in business.

An alternative to merging is for struggling schools to enter into collaborative working arrangements with others. This allows the schools to retain their independent legal identities, but to save costs by working together on aspects of their operational activities. For example, the shared use of facilities or outsourcing of functions, including financial reporting, information systems or payroll services could result in significant savings.

Provided that the Charity Commission is satisfied that the schools' governing bodies, as charity trustees, are acting in the best interests of their schools and that they have properly assessed the risks and benefits of the arrangement, it may be able to assist the parties by amending their constitutions (where necessary) to enable the collaboration.

Mergers?

Nonetheless, a few institutions may find themselves unable to continue independently as going concerns. Their interests may be better served by seeking a merger with other schools, rather than taking the decision to close. There are, currently, signs that the growth in merger activity will accelerate. Schools facing the greatest challenges are girls' boarding schools and boarding prep schools.

A merger can be effected by two or more schools transferring their property and assets into an entirely new entity or by one organisation taking over the business of the other.

A merger should not be rushed into. Where mistakes happen, they usually occur at the outset. A merger's cost in both fiscal and reputational terms should not be underestimated. Professional advice should be taken if a merger is proposed. As with collaborative working arrangements, there are legal and best practice considerations that must be taken into account before action can be taken. The usual requirements of compatibility of purpose and of the governors having the requisite powers to merge will take precedence.

Less happy are the cases where mergers have been poorly managed by governing bodies that have lacked the strategic foresight and courage to take big decisions.

Major factors to consider as part of this process will include:
- the geographical locations of the merging schools;
- their respective demographic constitution and the demographic trends; and

- anticipated local authority planning developments of the areas in which each is based.

The causes of mergers and closures

Most recent mergers and closures have been caused by combinations of tougher markets, changing attitudes to single-sex education, debates about the best age to start boarding, falling rolls, demographics, improved choice for parents, not least from the maintained sector, and the rising level of fees. These factors need to be recognised and addressed promptly and effectively. But can heads speak easily about these points at times of stress? This situation is not always helped when a significant proportion of governors are old boys or old girls with affection for the "old ways" of the school.

The merging schools should assess what assets, liabilities and property will be transferred and whether any of the assets or property will be held as permanent endowment or on other special trusts that might prevent them being amalgamated with those of the recipient charity or sold.

The sale of property (in accordance with charity law) or assets may raise extra finance to fund the continued operation of the merged school, but Charity Commission involvement will be required where there is permanent endowment.

Understanding parents

Parents will inevitably be upset by a perceived threat to their children's education, particularly if crucial exams are looming. Also, they may be alarmed at the potential disturbance that may be caused to the emotional security of the children. This may be felt particularly keenly in the event of a closure. Schools must ensure that they have prepared for this. For example, they could contact other schools with a similar culture, that cover a similar syllabus and that would be interested in taking pupils, and arranging an open day for parents to talk to other schools about opportunities.

Governors have a crucial part to play here. Not only is it their role to direct the merger or closure discussions, but they also need to be aware of the pressure that will be created. Parents will often focus their anxieties and concerns on the head, albeit that it is unlikely to have been her or his decision.

Practical support for staff

Similarly, the head and governors should also be worried about the welfare of staff, as well as having to deal with media representatives: all this, at a time when their own future may be in doubt. Another key and inevitable cost-saving measure during a merger is the redundancy of some staff. It is essential that the legal and contractual consultations and procedures are followed. An incorrectly handled redundancy can prove expensive in compensation paid to those made redundant and of adverse impact on reputation.

Governors must lead the way
Governors need to be proactive in these aspects of the merger or closure. In addition to their legal and administrative concerns, it is imperative that the interests of parents, pupils and staff are not forgotten. A strategy that is inclusive of all stakeholders should be the best guarantee of a successful implementation. Above all, they must establish a close, confidential steering group, including the head, to determine strategy and tactics.

Vetting and barring, by Andrew Maiden
The Vetting and Barring Scheme safeguards came into effect in October 2009. They were established as a result of the Bichard enquiry (launched in response to the Soham murders) that recommended that anyone who works with youngsters should be registered. It is a partnership between the Independent Safeguarding Authority (ISA) and the Criminal Records Bureau (CRB). It is supported in law by the Safeguarding Vulnerable Groups Act 2006 (in England and Wales) and the Safeguarding Vulnerable Groups Order in Northern Ireland.

The lists that have barred individuals from working with youngsters (Protection of Children Act List, Protection of Vulnerable Adults List and List 99 in England and Wales) have been replaced by two new lists administered by the ISA. Monitoring of the lists is carried out by the CRB.

Anyone who works or volunteers with children and vulnerable adults will be legally required to be registered with the ISA. Individuals can register from July 2010.

Limited options
Schools can only allow ISA-registered people to carry out "regulated activities". Governors come under this category. Where governors are volunteers, registration is free.

A person's ISA status must be checked before employing them, whether in a paid capacity or as a volunteer. Schools cannot take their word for it and allow them to start work in the school, even supervised, before the outcome of the check. Enhanced CRB checks must be carried out on all school staff.

The ISA assesses the risk of harm that an individual might pose to vulnerable groups (ie pupils), based on information held about that person. Sources of information include the police, local authorities and employers.

When a person becomes ISA-registered, they will be monitored and their status will be reassessed as new information about them comes to light. Employers (ie schools) can register an interest to be kept abreast of an employee's change of status. Employers that engage someone they know to be barred will be committing an offence.

Scotland has its own vetting and barring scheme, but the two schemes will share information and recognise each other's bars.

School protection guidance, by Andrew Maiden
In June 2008, a school's head was accused of harming pupils and lowering educational and welfare standards. Governors failed to act, so the Charity Commission stepped in and opened a statutory inquiry.

Findings concluded that the governing body should have suspended the head. Despite advice from the commission that it should have done so, it considered the allegations to be unfounded, so failed to act.

In response, the commission issued an s.19A direction to ensure that the governors monitored the head's performance during investigations. The governing body also failed to comply with the direction. Governors did not have an appropriate complaints procedure in place. During the inquiry, parents registered complaints that were not processed by the governing body.

The governing body was subsequently found not to be acting in the charity's best interests.

Commission ruling
The commission insisted that the governing body undertook a complete governance review. In future, the school must respond quickly to complaints, ensure that adequate complaints procedures are in place, that clear lines of accountability have been drawn and that pupils' best interests are always at the heart of decision-making.

Any charity with an income of more than £25,000 is required to confirm in its annual return that there have been no incidents over the previous year that have come to the attention of the Charity Commission.

Handling a crisis, by Alistair Macdonald
In the event of a crisis, schools must be quick to manage the inevitable media intrusion. Unless handled carefully and actively, you risk allowing your school's exposure to turn into a media disaster.

In 2008, a respected independent school in the north of England rebuffed media enquiries when details of a new teacher's former career emerged on the internet. A deafening silence from the headmaster and governors only served to intrigue and fascinate those in the media feeding-frenzy.

The school's lack of response overlooked the fact that the teacher's allegedly exotic past had come to light on a social networking site – posted by pupils. They were only too delighted to add their thoughts – and fantasies – while parents of pupils were equally willing to be interviewed. There was enough information available to provide any hack with oceans of salacious copy.

This episode displayed a worrying lack of understanding on the school's part of how the media works and of the pressures new technology has created. Not talking to journalists won't magic away comment or criticism.

A plan of action
Most independent schools have a reasonably robust crisis plan – but with one yawning gap. In the section marked Handling the Media, there are one-liners such as: "We don't talk to the press" or "Only the headteacher gives media interviews". No matter how good your crisis plan is, your school's reputation is at stake if you don't handle the media carefully and deal with their legitimate enquiries.

Saying "no comment" – whether directly or implicitly – is not effective. If journalists can't get a response to their questions, then they will speculate and some will even, regrettably, make up the details. You may not like it, but it happens and there's nothing new about it.

Faster and more
What is new is the shape of the media today. New technology has revolutionised the printing industry. The tediously slow process of hot metal printing has given way to flexible and fast digital printing. During the same period, the number of radio stations has proliferated from fewer than ten to more than 800. And you can now access around 500 TV stations in the UK.

If you think this is rapid change, just consider the impact of the mobile phone and the internet on newsgathering. You can get live pictures from the summit of Mt Everest, from the Titanic thousands of feet down on the seabed, and even from the moon.

News delivery is now instantaneous. It is sobering to recall that mobile phone pictures of the London 7/7 bombings were posted on the internet for the whole world to see within a couple of minutes. The sheer speed of modern communications makes news management difficult – but not impossible if you take control.

The drowning of a 17-year-old pupil on a school trip to Ecuador two years ago underscores this point. The story was making headlines in online news bulletins within hours. But open and honest handling of the media by the school and the adventure travel company running the trip – their first tragedy in 21 years in business – hugely enhanced the reputations of both. News coverage was positive despite a mildly critical remark made by the coroner at the subsequent inquest.

So where do these developments leave independent schools? You need to raise your game to cope with these new challenges. Schools must prepare well, practise their media responses and be prepared to keep an arm's length but meaningful relationship with the media.

Why you?
But why are journalists so fascinated with independent schools anyway? The answer is that reporters are always interested in something that is different to the norm – that's what news is. It's new. The politics of envy also plays a part. People love to see the seemingly privileged under the cosh – quietly overlooking the growing number of bursary places and the fact that many parents of independently educated children have made lifestyle choices to ensure school fees for academic excellence are a priority.

Is it worth it?
But why should you bother with the media? There is a harsh reality to this. The independent schools sector is a competitive marketplace. High academic standards are usually a given, so parents make their choice of school on other criteria. Many will base their decisions on the quality of extracurricular activities, sporting excellence or good pastoral care. Extracurricular activities top this list, in my view.

Independent schools are virtually the last outpost of interesting school trips, adventure activities and life-enhancing risk-taking. But accidents, injuries, misdemeanours and – sometimes – a death make good copy. Handle these stories well and your school's reputation will be enhanced; handle them badly and parents of prospective pupils may decide to entrust the care of their offspring to apparently more caring or responsible hands.

Seven ways
Managing your reputation through the media is critical; it makes sound commercial sense. Here are seven secrets of successful crisis news management:
- never speculate or apportion blame: your insurers won't like it and the true cause of an accident may be unexpected;
- never name victims: unless you have absolutely rock-solid confirmation that police have informed next-of-kin;
- never embroider: keep interviews short and simple. You need to provide a few basic facts to prevent the more disreputable hacks from making up a story, but you should not be in the business of writing a reporter's story for her or him;
- never say "no comment": you'll sound guilty even if you're innocent. And don't raise your voice or appear rattled;

- stay calm;
- always keep promises to the media: such as the timing of news releases and interviews. Not understanding their deadlines will only antagonise them; and
- always be human and sympathetic: a crisis involving children requires tact and understanding.

Always tell the truth: a few white lies may come back to haunt you. Ask Jeffrey Archer. But, don't say too much too soon – be guided by legal advice and your insurers. Follow these guidelines and you can help prevent your school crisis turning into a disaster.

Chapter **9**

Useful contacts for more information

Association of Governing Bodies of Independent Schools
www.agbis.info

Association for Marketing & Development in Independent Schools
www.amdis.co.uk

Boarding Schools' Association
www.boarding.org.uk

Bridge Schools Inspectorate
www.bridgeschoolsinspectorate.co.uk

Catholic Independent Schools' Conference
www.cisc.eteach.com

Charity Commission
www.charity-commission.gov.uk

Council of British International Schools
www.cobis.org.uk

Department for Education
www.education.gov.uk

Education and Training Inspectorate (inspections in Northern Ireland)
www.etini.gov.uk

Estyn (inspections in Wales)
www.estyn.gov.uk

Girls' Schools Association
www.gsa.uk.com

Headmasters' and Headmistresses' Conference
www.hmc.org.uk

HM Inspectorate of Education (inspections in Scotland)
www.hmie.gov.uk

Independent Association of Prep Schools
www.iaps.org.uk

Independent Safeguarding Authority
www.isa-gov.org.uk

Independent School Awards
www.fisawards.co.uk

Independent Schools Association
www.isaschools.org.uk

Independent Schools Council
www.isc.co.uk

Independent Schools Inspectorate
www.isi.net

Independent Schools' Bursars Association
www.theisba.org.uk

Ofsted
www.ofsted.gov.uk

Scottish Council of Independent Schools
www.scis.org.uk

Society of Heads of Independent Schools
www.shmis.org.uk

Index

Notes

Notes

Notes

Contributors (in alphabetical order)

Con Alexander is a charities partner at Veale Wasbrough Lawyers. Con can be contacted on **CAlexander@VWL.CO.UK**

Anita Bird is a consultant for Octagon Human Resources. Anita can be contacted on **anita@octagonhr.co.uk**

Ben Brice is a solicitor at Bircham Dyson Bell LLP. Ben can be contacted on **benbrice@bdb-law.co.uk**

Bill Brown is chairman of the Education Partnership and a governor at Kings' School, Winchester. Bill can be contacted on **billbrown@edpa.org.uk**

Penny Chapman is a partner at Bircham Dyson Bell LLP. Penny can be contacted on **pennychapman@bdb-law.co.uk**

Noble Hanlon is a partner at haysmacintyre. Noble can be contacted on **nhanlon@haysmacintyre.com**

Ewa Holender is a solicitor for Farrer & Co LLP. Ewa can be contacted on **exh@farrer.co.uk**

Susan Lawrence is a member of the national working party for business and enterprise, and is the headteacher of Kings' School, Winchester. Susan can be contacted on **kings.school@kings-winchester.hants.sch.uk**

Alistair Macdonald is a partner at Alexander Macdonald. Alistair can be contacted on **alistair@alexandermacdonald.co.uk**

Sam Macdonald is a partner at Farrer & Co LLP. Sam can be contacted on **shm@farrer.co.uk**

Simon Mackintosh is a partner and head of the charities team at Turcan Connell. Simon can be contacted on **sam@turcanconnell.com**

Andrew Maiden is editor of *Funding for Independent Schools* and *School Enterprise*. Andrew can be contacted on **andrew@pentastic.co.uk**

Anthony Millard is principal of Anthony Millard Consulting. Anthony can be contacted on **anthony@anthonymillard.co.uk**

Barney Northover is a partner at Veale Wasbrough Lawyers. Barney can be contacted on **BNorthover@VWL.CO.UK**

David Sewell is a partner at haysmacintyre. David can be contacted on **dsewell@haysmacintyre.com**

Nick Sladden is a partner in Baker Tilly. Nick can be contacted on **nick.sladden@bakertilly.co.uk**

Tracey Young is a partner at haysmacintyre. Tracey can be contacted on **tyoung@haysmacintyre.com**

The publishers would like to thank all contributors for their expert advice and guidance.

Insurance for schools

Governors of a school, have a duty to safeguard the property of the school from not only direct loss and damage but also from third party liabilities which would otherwise have to be satisfied out of the property of the school. Should governors fail to discharge this duty satisfactorily, they could be personally liable to make good the losses incurred by the school. Arranging appropriate property and liability insurance is a means of discharging this duty.

Set out below are a few general points which should be considered when arranging insurance.

Get the right level of cover and make sure it includes.....

a waiver of the condition of average. Commercial insurance policies will often include as standard the 'pro-rata condition of average' which means that any underinsurance within the policy will be penalised by reducing claims settlements in proportion with the level of underinsurance. Check if your broker or insurer is able to offer a professional building valuation whereby, if the resulting sums insured are accepted by the school, the insurer should then be able to offer you a guarantee that the pro-rata condition of average will not apply in the event of a loss.

When considering new insurance providers, avoid at all costs.....

accepting a quotation purely on cost alone. If you obtain alternative quotations to your existing provider it is important to review not only the premiums being quoted but also the level of cover being offered to ensure that the interests of both the school and its governors are fully protected. Important areas to assess are the limits of indemnity for employers' liability, public liability and governor's liability, the claims excess levels, your business interruption indemnity period and the extent of the personal accident cover for your staff, governors and voluntary helpers.

Always ensure.....

that all material facts are disclosed to the insurer via your broker (if you are using one). Every proposer or insured, when seeking new insurance or amending or renewing an existing policy must disclose any information which might influence the insurer in deciding whether or not to accept the risk, what the terms policy should be or what premium to charge. If you fail to disclose all material facts, this may render the insurance voidable from inception (the start of the contract) and enable the insurer to repudiate liability (entitle the insurer not to pay your claims). If you are not sure whether a fact is material you should disclose it.

Don't forget to check.....

what services are included within your premiums. It is important to check that there are no hidden costs during the insurance period for services such as negotiations with insurers (where cover is arranged via a broker) and additional visits to the school by an account manager. Your insurer or advisor should also provide you with continuous administration and support, on-going market advice and perhaps, most importantly, risk management advice and assistance where required. It is important to be clear that these are all included within any premiums or fees and indeed that these services are being provided at all.

Marsh Ltd, Education Practice, Capital House, 1-5 Perrymount Road, Haywards Heath, West Sussex RH16 3SY
Telephone: 01444 458144 Facsimile: 01444 415088 Web: www.marsh.co.uk

Other reviews of
The **Independent School Governor's** Handbook:

"An invaluable guide for prospective governors, and a concise checklist for experienced ones."
Nigel Richardson, former chairman of HMC and former head of the Perse School

"A good, comprehensive document."
Giles Bowring, bursar, Giggleswick School

"Andrew Maiden, who edits and publishes the very useful *Funding for Independent Schools* magazine, has identified a gap in the market for this book. It is packed with best practice advice. More importantly, it has a number of essays on effective independent school governance which I would commend to any governor, head or bursar."
Clive Gutteridge, bursar, Appleford School

The Independent School Governor's Handbook is published by the team behind *Funding for Independent Schools*, the leading magazine for heads and bursars of independent schools in the UK. The magazine covers the key strategic, financial and fundraising issues to keep the independent schools sector viable.

© pentastic ltd November 2009
ISBN 978-0-9563092-0-4